The HITLER File

C.A.R. Hills

Batsford Academic and Educational Limited

REICHSKANZLER
ADOLF HITLER

File notes on Adolf Hitler

1	FAMILY NAME	CHRISTIAN NAME
	Hitler	Adolf

2	NATIONALITY
	Austrian until 1932, then German

3	PLACE OF BIRTH	4	DATE OF BIRTH
	Braunau am Inn, Austria		20 April 1889

5	PLACE OF DEATH	6	DATE OF DEATH
	Berlin, Germany		30 April 1945

7	FATHER	8	MOTHER
	Alois Hitler, civil servant, died 1903		Klara Pölzl Hitler, housewife, died 1908

9	BROTHERS AND SISTERS
	A sister, a half brother and a half sister lived to adulthood

10	MARITAL DETAILS
	Married Eva Braun, 29 April 1945

11	CHILDREN
	None

12 DESCRIPTION (AT 50 YEARS)

HEIGHT	BUILD	HAIR	WEIGHT	EYES
5ft 9 ins	Average	Brown to black hair, forelock over left temple. Moustache	about 150 lbs	Light blue flecked with greenish grey

13	PECULIARITIES
	Nervous tic. Eyes of hypnotic power.

14 MAJOR POLITICAL/MILITARY POSTS HELD

Führer of Nazi Party, 1921-1945
Chancellor of German Reich, 1933-1945
President of German Reich, 1934-1945
German dictator, 1933-1945

First published 1980
© text C.A.R. Hills 1980
Typeset by Tek-Art Ltd S.E.20
Printed in Hong Kong
for the Publishers,
Batsford Academic and Educational Limited,
4 Fitzhardinge Street, London W1H 0AH

ISBN 0 7134 1919 9

Acknowledgment

The Author and Publishers thank the following for their permission to use the pictures in this book: BBC Hulton Picture Library, for figs 11, 20, 39, 43 46, 47, 53; Imperial War Museum, for figs 9, 41, 42, 50; Popperfoto, for the frontispiece and figs 1, 2, 3, 4, 5, 6, 7, 8, 10, 12, 13, 14, 15, 16, 17, 18, 19, 21, 22, 23, 24, 25, 26, 27, 28, 29, 30, 31, 32, 33, 34, 35, 36, 37, 38, 40, 44, 45, 48, 49, 51, 54, 55; John Topham Picture Library, for fig 52. Thanks are expressed also to Peta Hambling for the picture research on this book.

Frontispiece: Hitler posing as the dynamic Führer of the German people.

Contents

Introduction

Adolf Hitler, ruler of Germany between 1933 and 1945, was a unique political leader. He is the dominant figure in twentieth-century European history, the greatest conqueror of all world history, and a ruler of such ruthlessness that his very name has become a byword for evil.

But Hitler was unusual as a leader in other ways too. Most political leaders, unless they have won power through having first been soldiers, are dedicated politicians all their lives. They spring from movements that existed before them, make a contribution to their movement, and leave political heirs to carry on their work. This is not the case with Hitler. His life, which lasted only fifty-six years, divided, in fact, into two almost equal parts: an earlier period when he was a mere nobody, drifting and unsuccessful, at one time even a homeless tramp; and a second period when almost single-handed he created his own movement, the Nazi party, became leader of his country, conquered a vast empire and, after this amazing success, led his people to total defeat and himself committed suicide. The extraordinary contrast between the two periods was not owing to any great change in Hitler's ideas or personality during his lifetime. Rather, in a period of great disturbance, frustration and uncertainty for the German people, this strange man, a mixture of the conventional and the unbalanced, a brilliant politician who was also almost a psychopath, seemed to express their deepest hopes and fears. Many people have noticed how much Hitler simply represented hidden urges and frustrations of his people. And Hitler himself used this fact in his propaganda, because his aim was to convince the German people that he was the heaven-sent answer to their problems. Thus in one of his speeches when he was leader he said:

> In Germany bayonets do not terrorize a people. Here a government is supported by the confidence of the entire people. I care for the people. In fifteen years I have slowly worked my way up together with this movement. I have not been imposed by anyone upon this people. From the people I have grown up, in the people I have remained, to the people I return. My pride is that I know no statesman in the world who with greater right than I can say that he is the representative of his people.

But we must remember that this is propaganda, whatever truth it may contain. If Hitler was the product of his nation's history, he also belonged to a brief, unusual and catastrophic period of it. And if he was in some ways a man in the crowd, he was also a brilliant politician, a hysterical personality,

1 Hitler "blesses" a Nazi Party standard by touching it with the "Blood Flag" carried at the Putsch of 1923.

and a leader who disregarded what for centuries had been regarded as decent standards in political life.

It is almost certain that in the conditions of the 1920s in Germany — the aftermath of defeat in war, an unstable democracy, roaring inflation, economic depression — a movement like the Nazi Party was bound to become powerful and probably some sort of dictatorship would have arisen anyway. But Hitler's personality brought to the movement that did arise an immense dynamism, almost

limitless ambition, and a willingness to encourage the most barbaric methods. To take but one example: the crime for which the Nazi regime will always be most notorious, the murder of six million Jews, was very much a personal project of Hitler's and the result of his teaching. In his propaganda Hitler also used the fact that he was a unique individual and claimed he had a semi-divine mission to save his people:

However weak the individual may be when compared with the omnipotence and will of Providence, yet at the moment when he acts as Providence would have him act he becomes immeasurably strong. Then there streams down upon him that force which has marked all greatness in the world's history. And when I look back only on the five years which lie behind us, then I feel justified in saying: This has not been the work of man alone.

Hitler said this in 1937 when he was at the height of his success and was beginning to feel that his powers were practically super-human. The next eight years were to show that he could, after all, be defeated, but at a cost of many millions of lives. The purpose of this book will be to try to understand this extraordinary leader both as a unique individual and as the product of a tragic and bloody era in history.

Chapter One 1889-1918

Hitler's Formative Years

Hitler's background

Hitler's ancestors had been Austrian peasants for hundreds of years, but his father, Alois Hitler, had by ability and hard work become a member of the lower middle class, a customs official of the Austro-Hungarian empire which was the government in the area until the revolution of 1918. Hitler's ancestors on both sides came from the Waldviertel, a poor, remote, heavily wooded district between the Danube and what is now Czechoslovakia and the Bavarian region of Germany. He himself was born on 20 April 1889 in Braunau am Inn, a small town very close to the German frontier, a fact to which he was to attach great importance when he began to see it as his mission to lead the Austrian and all other Germanic peoples into a new empire, the "thousand year Reich". There is no real truth in the legend that Hitler's real name was Schicklgruber. Hitler's father, Alois, was illegitimate, but his grandmother, whose maiden name was Schicklgruber, later married the man, a wandering miller, who was presumed to be the father of her child, and Alois took his name of Hiedler or Hitler. Adolf Hitler was never known by any other name; the other name was dug up by his enemies to make him look ridiculous.

Alois Hitler was in many ways a typical Austro-Hungarian customs official, authori-tarian, harsh and a little unsympathetic, it seems, towards his children: Hitler's earliest years were dominated by conflict with him

2 Hitler as a baby.

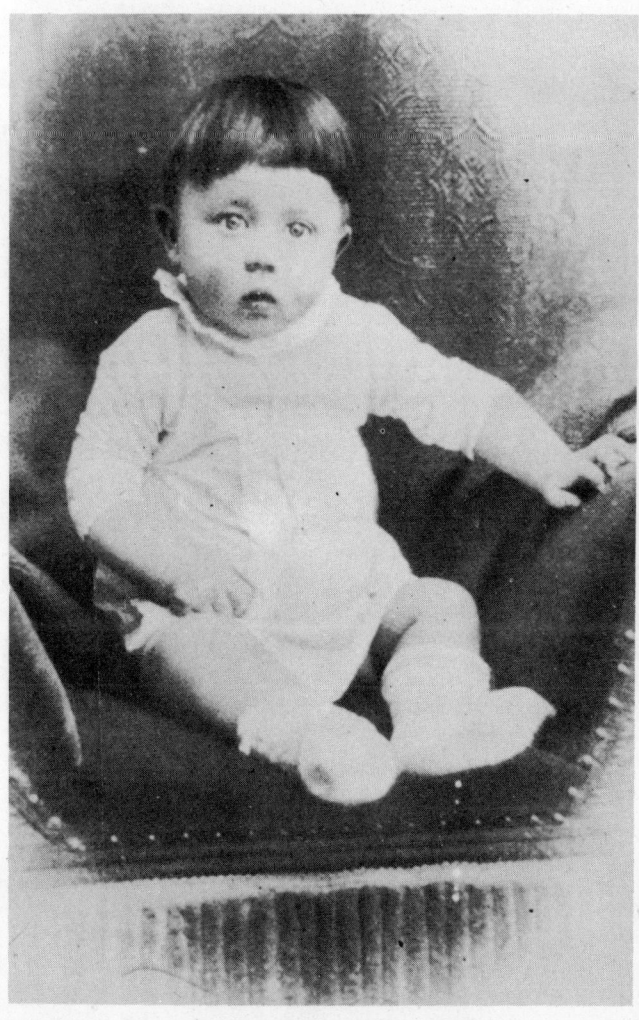

and by love of his mother, born Klara Pölzl, a gentle and pious woman who called her son *"mondsüchtig"* (moonstruck). Hitler grew into a headstrong and moody boy who rejected what he saw as his father's boring way of life and developed dreams of becoming a famous man and an artist. In adulthood Hitler had this to say about the conflict between him and his father:

> I did not want to become a civil servant, no, and again no. All attempt on my father's part to inspire me with love or pleasure in this profession by stories from

3 Alois Hitler, the stern, strict customs official of ▷ the Austro-Hungarian empire.

4 Klara Pölzl Hitler, a gentle, retiring woman to whom her son was close.
▽

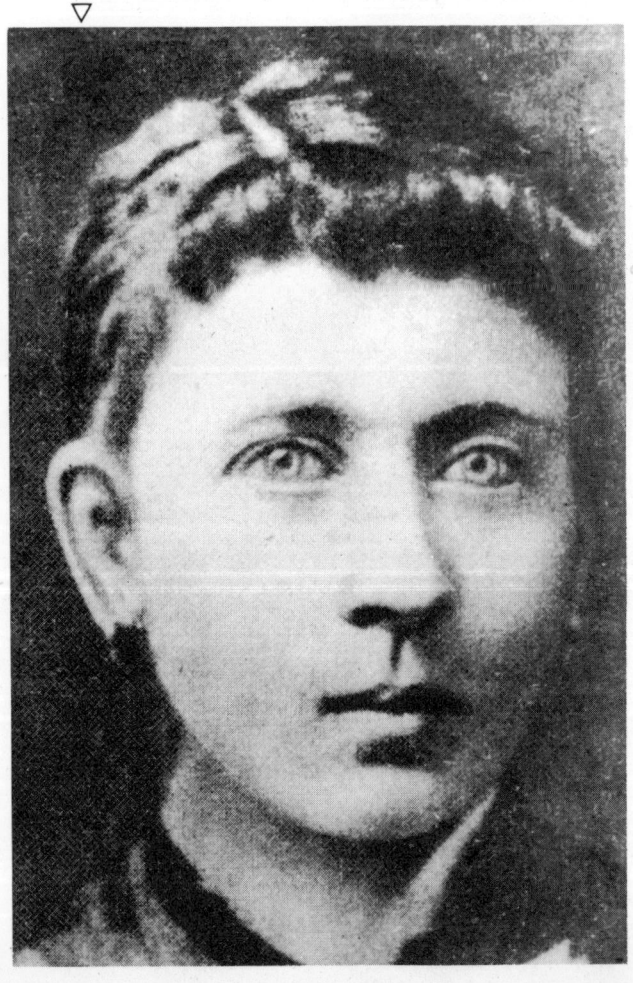

his own life accomplished the exact opposite . . . . One day it became clear to me that I would become a painter, an artist . . . . My father was struck speechless . . . "Artist! No! Never as long as I live!" . . . My father would never depart from his "Never!" And I intensified my "Nevertheless!"

At school too Hitler showed this headstrong character and there began a history of failure which was to be the pattern of his youth. One of his teachers, Eduard Hümer, gave this description of the schoolboy Hitler just before his trial for treason, twenty-five years later in 1923:

I can recall the gaunt, pale-faced youth pretty well. He had definite talent, though in a narrow field. But he lacked self-discipline, being notoriously cantankerous, wilful, arrogant and bad-tempered. He had

5 Hitler (marked with a cross) with his class at elementary school.

obvious difficulty in fitting in at school. Moreover he was lazy . . . his enthusiasm for hard work evaporated all too quickly. He reacted with ill-concealed hostility to advice or reproof; at the same time, he demanded of his fellow pupils their unqualified subservience, fancying himself in the role of leader . . .

Much of the later Hitler is already present in this description, Hitler showed interest in some subjects at school, especially history and geography, but could not settle down and finally left school at sixteen without a leaving certificate. He only ever had anything good to say about one of his teachers, Dr Leopold Pötsch, a fanatical German nationalist who had a great influence on him: there is an atmosphere of nationalist extremism about Hitler even from his earliest days.

Alois Hitler had died in 1903. Having left school Adolf continued to live at home with his mother, doing very little and indulging his dreams of becoming an architect. They now lived in the provincial town of Linz and Hitler whiled away the time in libraries and at the opera, already interested in the operas of Richard Wagner which celebrated German heroes. He had one friend called August Kubizek, the son of a Linz upholsterer, and he provided a willing audience for the adolescent Hitler's youthful dreams, frustrations and growing hatred of the society which he felt might reject him. One evening, Kubizek recalls, they went to hear Wagner's opera *Rienzi*. The opera concerns a medieval Roman noble who became a great leader of his people. After the opera ended the two young men went for a walk in the darkness on the hills above Linz, and then Hitler told his friend that he would be, not an artist, but a great leader of the German people:

> Words burst from him like a backed-up flood breaking through crumbling dams. In grandiose, compelling images, he sketched for me his future and that of his people.

These words were not to bear fruit for many years. The immediate problem for the young Hitler was how he was to make his living or what career he should follow; there were no political opportunities for him in the stifling, class-conscious atmosphere of the ancient Austro-Hungarian empire. But when he met Kubizek again thirty years later when he was German leader and they recalled their conversation, Hitler said to him: "It began at that hour!"

The Vienna years

Adolf Hitler went to live in Vienna, the capital of the Austro-Hungarian empire, in

6 Adolf Hitler, aged sixteen, sketched by his schoolfriend, August Kubizek.

the autumn of 1907, and he lived there, except for very brief intervals, for the next six years. It was, in many ways, the most formative period of his life. In Vienna Hitler learnt to hate.

He still had no job when he went there, and his initial ambition in going was to enter the Academy of Fine Arts and thereby become a famous artist or architect. But when he made his first attempt the Classification list contained the following entry:

> The following took the test with insufficient results or were not admitted . . . .
> Adolf Hitler, Braunau a. Inn, 20th April 1889.
> German. Catholic. Father, civil servant. 4 classes in *Realschule*.* Few heads. Test drawing unsatisfactory.

Hitler tried again, but was again unsuccessful. It was a terrible shock. His mother died in 1908 and for a while Hitler could live on her savings and on his orphan's pension. He continued to live the life of an "art student" and to drift aimlessly.

By 1909 his money had run out and he was forced to leave the furnished room which he had been renting. For a while Hitler, whose father had so proudly climbed into the ranks of the middle classes, became a tramp wandering the streets. When winter came he was able to find a temporary refuge in a doss-house, and he later moved into a hostel or "home for men" where he could live more permanently and where he in fact stayed for the rest of his time in Vienna, until 1913. Hitler later wrote with personal feeling about the type of boy who comes from the country to the city but fails to adjust to its demands:

> He loiters about and is hungry. Often he pawns or sells the last of his belongings.

*A type of school for less academically gifted or less well-off pupils.

His clothes begin to get shabby — with the increasing poverty of his outward appearance he descends to a lower social level.

A fellow-tramp, a man called Hanisch, later described his first meeting with Hitler in the Vienna doss-house in 1909:

> On the very first day there sat next to the bed that had been allotted to me a man who had nothing on except an old torn pair of trousers — Hitler. His clothes were being cleaned of lice, since for days he had been wandering about without a roof and in a terribly neglected condition.

The two unfortunates joined forces in looking for work; on more than one occasion they swept snow from the streets. Later they hit on the idea that Hitler would paint post-cards which Hanisch would then sell. They then had a rather undignified quarrel over the proceeds which led to Hitler's taking out a lawsuit against his partner who consequently spent a week in jail.

In 1913 Hitler left Vienna for Munich in Germany. The reason was to escape military service in the Austro-Hungarian empire, but it was not for cowardice. He had come to loathe the society of Vienna and had made the decision to commit himself to Germany: a private decision, but also his first important political decision and the start of a new life. He desperately needed a purpose in life: the legend that he became a house painter is untrue, but the previous six years

7 A version of a Viennese church painted by Hitler in 1911 when he was living in a Vienna hostel. Probably sold for a few pence at the time, the painting was acquired by an art dealer in 1939 for twenty thousand dollars "as an investment".
▽

8 Hitler sent this postcard of the scene he had ▷ painted to his friend Kubizek.

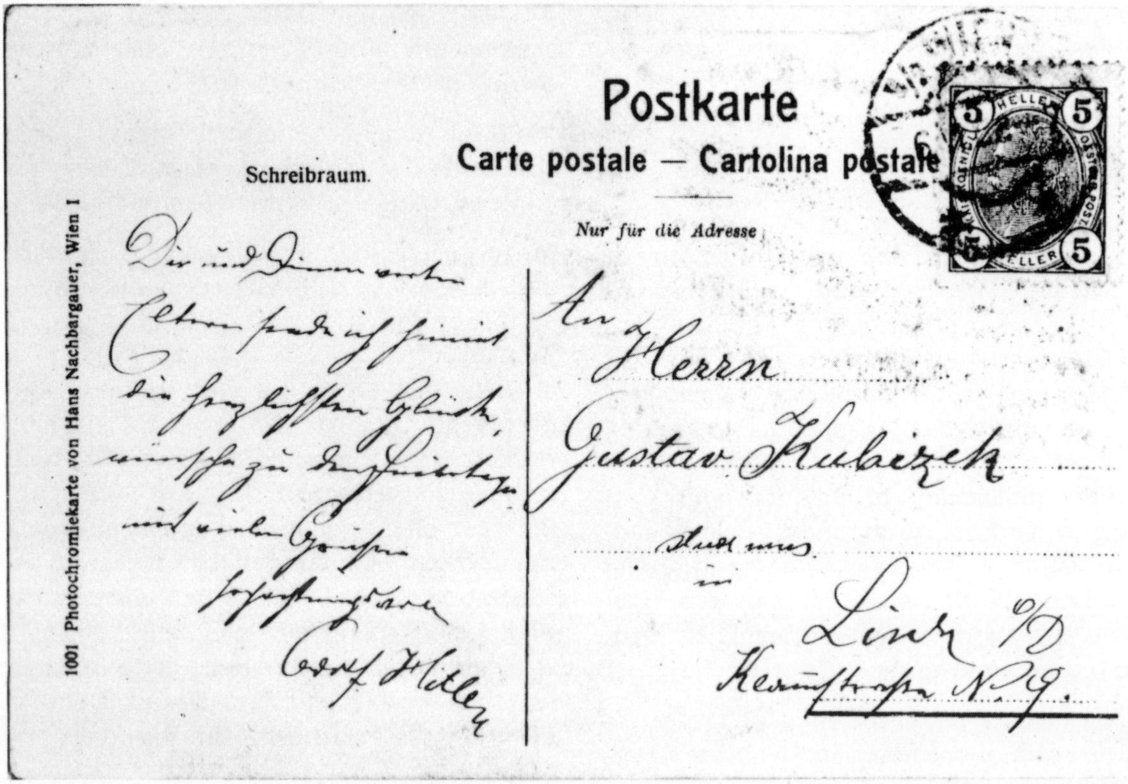
Postkarte

Carte postale — Cartolina postale

Schreibraum.

Nur für die Adresse

1001 Photochromiekarte von Hans Nachbargauer, Wien I

Dir und Deinen werten Eltern sende ich hiemit die herzlichsten Glückwünsche zu den Feiertagen mit vielen Grüßen Hochachtungsvoll Adolf Hitler

An Herrn Gustav Kubizek stud. mus. in Linz a/D Klammstraße No. 9.

had spared him few other humiliations.

What did Hitler learn from those six years? He certainly did not learn to blame himself or his own fecklessness for his misfortunes: on the contrary, he was filled with self-pity and resentment against the world. But, unlike many other young men of this period who had suffered hardship, he did not turn to the idea of socialism with its vision of equality and brotherhood to comfort him. He felt too humiliated by his social downfall to have any fellow-feeling for the workers or their movement. Instead he developed what the historian Alan Bullock has called a "natural philosophy of the doss-house": a belief in hardness, ruthlessness, trickery and, above all, in struggle. Again and again during his lifetime Hitler spoke of life as a fight where any means or methods could be justified if they led to victory:

One creature drinks the blood of another.
The death of one nourishes the other. One
should not dribble about human feelings . . .
the struggle goes on.

Hitler always spoke with contempt of "human feelings" — love, self-sacrifice, honesty, friendship. Of the great virtues, courage was the only one he had time for. The supreme value for him was power, and this surely is the chief reason why his life produced nothing but destruction.

Hitler felt that he had lost his middle-class position during these years and he liked to dramatize himself throughout his life as an "artist" and rebel. But he retained a longing to be accepted by respectable people, even as he despised them. Thus, as a politician, he became a strange mixture of revolutionary and conservative, of the conventional and the extreme. He had read a lot, but not systematically and with a mind that rejected reason. Thus his ideas developed as an appalling hotch-potch of what was considered "thought" in Viennese cafés and beer-halls at this period, carried to their extreme by a man looking for someone to fight. He adopted the crude

racialism and the blind belief in authority that he saw around him. He once summed up his beliefs very succinctly:

All life is bound up in three theses: struggle
is the father of all things, virtue lies in
blood, leadership is primary and decisive.

Many people in the German-speaking world also believed or half-believed in these things at this period and Hitler was only unusual in the lengths he was prepared to go to in applying his ideas. He was to find many people to support him in even his most ruthless crimes, most of them more unthinking than ill-intentioned.

Above all, Hitler needed an enemy: something to pin his intense burden of hatred and frustration to. His belief was in the superiority of the Germans in race and blood, and so it was natural that he should come to intensely hate the people who could most easily be identified as "outsiders" in society — the Jews.

In Germany itself many of the Jews were rich and educated people, but in Vienna they were mainly new immigrants from eastern Europe, strange in their manners and speech, arriving in large numbers. Hitler described the feelings he developed about the Jews in obscene and violent language:

Was there any shady undertaking, any form
of foulness, especially in cultural life, in
which at least one Jew did not participate?
On putting the probing knife carefully to
that kind of abscess one immediately discovered, like a maggot in a putrescent
body, a little Jew who was often blinded
by the sudden light.

This really is the voice of the gutter: it was later to become the voice of the man who ruled all Europe. The question remains:

9   Hitler stands, an unknown man, in the enthusiastic crowd greeting the announcement of war in 1914 in the Odeonsplatz in Munich

which was the sicker, Hitler or the world that let him come into power?

The move to Munich and the coming of the war

Hitler moved to Munich in May 1913 and took lodgings with a tailor's family in a poor quarter near the barracks. In later years he was to say that moving across the frontier to a city in Germany made a great difference to his happiness, but he continued in the same drifting way making a precarious living selling pictures and illustrated postcards.

War broke out in Europe in early August 1914. The two powers where the ruling class were Germans — the German empire and the Austro-Hungarian empire — were pitted against the Russian empire, France and Britain. All three eastern European empires were to be destroyed by this war, but neither the cheering crowds in the streets nor their aristocratic rulers had any inkling of this. Hitler, who listened in the crowd in the Odeonsplatz in Munich to the news of war, was among the most enthusiastic. Here at last was a purpose in life. To Hitler the war was:

a case of Germany fighting for her own existence — the German nation for its own to be or not to be, for its freedom and for its future. . . . For me, as for every other German, the most memorable

period of my life now began. Face to face with that mighty struggle all the past fell away into oblivion.

Historians are now agreed that the First World War, like the Second, was largely caused by German desires for expansion in Europe and was thus hardly a case of "Germany fighting for her own existence", but this fact was only likely to increase the enthusiasm of a man such as Hitler. Although still an Austrian national, he made a personal application to the Bavarian King (who still remained as a local ruler in the German empire) to be allowed to serve in a Bavarian and German regiment. This request was granted. In his book, *Mein Kampf* (My Struggle) Hitler describes his feelings on opening the letter of permission:

> I opened the document with trembling hands; no words of mine can describe the satisfaction I felt . . . . Within a few days I was wearing that uniform that I was not to put off again for nearly six years.

There now began for Hitler what he called "the greatest and most unforgettable time of my earthly existence".

Hitler as soldier

The List Regiment, which Hitler had joined, was sent to fight on the western front after only a few weeks of training in October 1914 and was almost immediately involved in the bloody first battle for Ypres. The war was a terrible experience for millions of men, very many of whom died, but for Hitler it was the first experience in his life of which he made at least a partial success. During the war he served as a courier (*Meldegänger*) between company headquarters and the front: not in the trenches, but a dangerous and responsible job. He was a brave soldier who received several decorations. But, in spite of this, he never advanced beyond the rank of corporal and, even considering the class-

consciousness of the German army, this is perhaps a little surprising. One reason why Hitler did not gain advancement seems to have been his reputation for eccentricity, fanaticism and an inability to mix much with his comrades. One of his fellow soldiers wrote of him:

> a peculiar fellow. He sat in the corner of our mess holding his head between his hands, in deep contemplation. Suddenly he would leap up, and, running about excitedly, say that in spite of our big guns victory would be denied us, for the invisible foes of the German people were a greater danger than the biggest cannon of the enemy.

The "invisible foes" Hitler meant were Jews and socialists. The photographs we have of Hitler from this period bear out this general impression of strangeness and brooding: deep eyes stare from a face that looks older than its years and contorted with seriousness.

Hitler was wounded in 1916 and sent to recover in Germany. While there, he became angry, contrasting the fighting spirit of the ordinary soldiers with the people complaining and making profits at home. He had no use, either for those who were trying to reach a compromise peace with the enemy:

> All decent men who had anything to say, said it point-blank in the enemy's face; or failing this, kept their mouths shut and did their duty elsewhere.

There was no room for independent thought in Hitler's world; he wanted merely struggle, obedience to authority and unquestioning faith. But this world was soon to be torn apart. In October 1918 the List Regiment found itself again near Ypres and there Hitler was badly wounded in a gas attack: he was temporarily blinded and, in this condition, he was sent back to a hospital in Germany.

10 Adolf Hitler (on the right) with two fellow soldiers photographed in 1916.

There, in November 1918, he received the news that Germany had surrendered to the hated enemy. Simultaneously he learnt that revolution had broken out among the workers in Germany. He described how he felt at that terrible moment:

> I could stand it no longer. It became impossible for me to sit still one minute more. Again everything went black before my eyes; I tottered and groped my way back to the dormitory, threw myself on my bunk, and dug my burning head into my blanket and pillow. Since the day I had stood at my mother's grave I had not wept . . . . But now I could not help it.

Like many other soldiers, Hitler could not accept that the magnificent German army had been fairly defeated on the field of battle: there had been, they believed, a "stab in the back" from traitors at home. The fact that, in reality, there had been almost no protest at home was not to alter this picture for Hitler or thousands like him. It became his mission now to root out the influence of these traitors, to punish them, and to both restore Germany to her former greatness and create a new and much greater destiny for her. Hitler was later to say that it was in the horror of that moment that he decided to enter politics.

Chapter Two 1919-1933

Leader in Waiting

The New World

The Germany into which Adolf Hitler emerged, now almost thirty, at the close of the war in 1918 was a world that suddenly had much more room for someone with his particular talents and aspirations.

The old Germany, ruled by aristocrats and the prosperous upper middle class, had collapsed under the pressures of war, and the German emperor, Wilhelm II, had been forced to go into exile in Holland. The social democrats, until recently treated as almost political outcasts (when Hitler was born they had actually been banned), were left in charge of the government in November 1918, to proclaim a republic, because none of the other parties wanted the responsibility.

Revolution was in the air: the new government quelled an attempted take-over by the more extreme socialists, the communists, in the early months of 1919. They did this with the aid of bands of returned soldiers who still wanted a military life and to quell the revolution. The soldiers were willing to cooperate with the new republican leaders to do this, but they had no loyalty to the new Weimar Republic. The new government, which had accepted responsibility in the hour of defeat, were sometimes referred to as "the November criminals".

The Versailles peace treaty, signed in June 1919, condemned Germany to lose territory and to pay heavy fines to the victorious powers of the First World War. The treaty caused a storm of protest in Germany and made the new republic even more unpopular. The economy was shaky and rapid inflation had already begun, which by 1922 was to reach catastrophic proportions. In 1920 a reactionary coup (attempt at take-over) by army leaders, aimed at restoring the empire, was only narrowly defeated. At the same time many middle-class people feared that the communists would take over and institute the same ruthless measures against the middle class as were being taken in newly communist Russia. Governments rose and fell, political murder became common, and a whole host of political movements sprang up, many composed of ex-soldiers, violent in their methods and often dedicated to extreme nationalistic and racist ideas.

This atmosphere of social crisis gave a new opportunity to people like Hitler who were prepared to become agitators. Hitler himself recognized this. He wrote of this period:

> I could not help but laugh at the thought of my own future which only a short time ago had given me such bitter concern.

It is certainly true that in the old world he would never have had the chance of becoming a political leader. But we must remember that at this period there were thousands of

local agitators like Hitler, many of them putting forward the same types of ideas. Only Hitler among them was to build up a powerful movement and with it take control of the country. This demonstrates that, although a man of drifting habits and crude ideas, he was also a political leader of great gifts, one who had a unique mixture of belief in his own mission and a cunning sense of political tactics and timing.

△

11 Friedrich Ebert (marked with a cross), new President of the German Republic, flanked by his government, proclaims the new German constitution in 1919.

12 The crew of a mine-thrower prepare to fire at a building held by communist revolutionaries in Berlin's Alexanderplatz in 1919.

Hitler finds his party

Immediately after the war ended, there was still no sign that Hitler had fundamentally changed his life-style. Like millions of other returned soldiers, his first impulse was to drift. On release from hospital he returned to Munich to report to the reserve battalion of his regiment, but he took no part in the turbulent events of the time in Munich, where an attempted communist take-over was in progress. For a while he got a job doing guard duty in a prisoner of war camp, but this was shortly closed down. He still had no thoughts of trying to make a regular living and wrote of this period:

At that time endless plans chased one another through my head. For days I wondered what could be done, but the end of every meditation was the sober realization that I, nameless as I was, did not possess the least basis for any useful action.

23

Thus spoke Hitler at thirty. It is difficult to avoid contrasting him with other political leaders. At that age Lenin, Stalin and Mao Tse-tung were already seasoned revolutionaries, Napoleon already ruler of France, Churchill already famous, Mussolini, the other important Fascist ruler, already editor of Italy's leading socialist newspaper. Hitler's coming to politics was very different: it was a very sudden finding of his latent powers in a situation where, equally suddenly, the world had become ready to take him seriously.

It happened in this way. He was given minor work in the army's political department and was sent to take a course in "civic thinking". While there, he discovered that he had a gift for making speeches: one of the most important discoveries of his life. He was given more work spreading nationalist propaganda among the soldiers and doing investigations into various political groups. In September 1919 he was sent to investigate a meeting of one of about fifty small right-wing parties and associations which had sprung up in Munich at that time: the German Workers' Party, run by a locksmith called Anton Drexler. At that time the party had only six committee members — and yet from that small nucleus the Nazi party was to spring. Hitler went to a party meeting at which one speaker demanded the separation of Bavaria from the rest of Germany. Hitler was so furious at this assault on the unity of Germany that he got to his feet and exercised his new-found talent for public speaking. He impressed the meeting so much that at the end he was handed a pamphlet by Drexler and a few days later received a postcard telling him that he had been elected a member and inviting him to a meeting of the small committee. After some hesitation he went. He described the scene he saw:

I went through the badly lighted guest-room, where not a single guest was to be seen, and searched for the door which led to the side room; and there I was face to face with the Committee. Under the dim light shed by a grimy gas-lamp I could see four people sitting around a table, one of them the author of the pamphlet.

Hitler joined; the party was indeed obscure but it offered him a chance to make his mark.

Hitler develops the Nazi party

Hitler was soon taking a leading role in the affairs of the new party. Before he joined, it had been more like a secret drinking society than a real political party, but Hitler now took a leading role in pushing it forward to more imaginative activity and bolder recruitment campaigns. In 1920 he was put in charge of the party's propaganda and began to organize mass meetings at which he himself spoke. He left the army and devoted all his time to building up the party. By 1921 he had ousted all rivals and was its acknowledged leader (*Führer*). He was determined that his will should be supreme and, indeed, power was never wrested from him, even when the German state lay in total ruins in 1945. More than any other leader in history, Hitler was the absolute final authority in his movement.

The original party founded by Drexler had been very confused in its ideas: a hotch-potch of nationalism and socialism. Drexler's original programme had been full of vague resentments against the upper classes, the working classes and the Jews, the hoarders and the rabble rousers. Happiness, said Drexler, lay not:

in talk and empty phrases in meetings, demonstrations and elections, but in good work, a full cook-pot and a fair chance for the children.

Hitler gave the party propaganda far more bite and provided it with a much tighter organization. In 1920 the name of the party was changed to the National Socialist German Workers' Party (NSDAP or Nazi for short). Under Hitler's leadership nationalism became more important in the party's philosophy than socialism. He concentrated the propaganda on demands for a return of German greatness, on hatred of the Jews and other racial enemies, and on a vision of a united community obeying a strong leader.

Through his speech-making Hitler began to discover his power of swaying a mass audience. He was a man who found it difficult to form relationships with individual people, but who had a magnetic power to sway a crowd. He spoke like this about his relationship with the masses:

Whoever wishes to win over the masses must know the key that will open the door to their hearts. It is not objectivity, which is a feckless attitude, but a determined will, backed up by power where necessary.

Hitler hammered home his simple, resentful message night after night in Bavarian beer-halls. He spoke about the need for strong, aggressive leaders and claimed that there was a Jewish-communist plot to destroy Germany. He also knew that in a disturbed situation the use of violence can be an asset in winning power. He organized bands of young fighting men who became the nucleus of a Nazi private army, the *Sturmabteilung* (storm-troopers) or SA. More people were impressed by the ability of the new party to beat its opponents up in the street than were frightened or repelled by it. Hitler devoted the utmost care to the symbols the party used — the swastika or hooked cross, the salute, the brown uniform of the stormtroopers, the rigid ranks of the party — all to build up an impression of strength and iron discipline.

These methods were successful and the party grew. It began to acquire powerful patrons and gifts of money, while Hitler was consulted by the other Bavarian politicians and army leaders. Hitler himself continued to live a rather drifting personal existence: no-one knew what money he lived on and it is still not clear. He was often seen in the streets carrying a rhinoceros-whip to create

an atmosphere of menace, but this did not totally hide a nervous tic and the remaining social uncertainty of someone who, not long before, had been an outcast wandering the streets. But in the changed circumstances the factors of personality that had hampered Hitler before did not seem to matter: they had almost become assets.

Hitler was now being joined by many of the men who were one day to help him rule Germany: Hermann Göring, the seedy aristocrat who was to later organize the *Luftwaffe* (Airforce), Ernst Röhm, the SA leader who was a valuable link with the army, Rudolf Hess, the most faithful follower who was to become deputy leader, as well as many other roughneck and even freakish personalities. By 1923 the party felt itself ready to make its first major bid for power.

The Beer-Hall Putsch

By 1923 the Weimar Republic had entered its period of deepest crisis. Inflation had reached such a pitch that overnight people's savings were worth nothing. The French armies were occupying the Ruhr area because Germany had not been able to pay the fines demanded of her after the war. There were communist uprisings, while in other parts of the country, especially in Bavaria, there was widespread agitation for separation from Germany.

Hitler planned to use this situation to seize a measure of power for his own still small party. He planned to start a Putsch (attempted take-over of government), using as temporary allies the local political leaders in Bavaria who wanted to revolt against the central government. He would then outwit and take power from these leaders and perhaps, if he had enough power behind him, march on Berlin and seize power there. It was an ambitious scheme which, given the power at Hitler's disposal at that moment, had little chance of success. The Bavarian leaders held a political meeting in a Munich beer-hall on

8 November 1923. Hitler and a band of Nazis turned up at the meeting (supported by the old war hero, General Ludendorff), and proceeded to virtually kidnap the leaders on the stage. Initially, however, the meeting seems to have been rather unimpressed by this drama: Hitler could be an impressive and frightening figure, but he quite often had a faint air of the ridiculous to him too. One of his patrons, Ernst Hanfstängl, a sophisticated half-American, described him at this period as being like:

> the slightly nervous sort of provincial bridegroom you can see in scores of pictures behind the dusty windows of Bavarian village photographers.

Hitler, however, managed to sway the meeting by making a brilliant speech in which he confidently proclaimed himself as head of a new government:

> The Bavarian ministry is removed. I propose that a Bavarian government shall be formed consisting of a Regent and a Prime Minister invested with dictatorial powers . . . . A new National Government will be nominated this very day, here in Munich. A German national army will be formed immediately . . . . I propose that until accounts have been finally settled with the November criminals, the direction of policy in the National Government be taken over by me.

This show of confidence swayed the meeting and the Bavarian leaders seemed to be agreeing to take part in this government. Then, by a bad error of judgement, Hitler left the hall without making sure that they were in Nazi custody and they managed to slip away. Without their support or any support from army units stationed nearby, the attempted take-over fizzled out within a single day. Not a single key position had been seized, while a few Nazis had been killed in a march they held through the city.

13 Hitler, in the overcoat, stands with the other accused at the time of his trial for treason. Ludendorff is next to Hitler (centre). Röhm is second right.

This attempt had shown that, in some ways, Hitler was an inexperienced politician. He was never to attempt this sort of midnight take-over again in his career. But his trial, which began in February 1924 and where he stood, with nine others, accused of treason, demonstrated how skilfully he could appeal to an audience. He treated his accusers with contempt and in his speeches almost managed to make it seem that it was they, not he, who were on trial:

> It is not you, gentlemen, who pass judgement on us. That judgement is spoken by the eternal court of history . . . . That court will judge us . . . as Germans who wanted only the good of their own people and Fatherland; who wanted to fight and die . . . the goddess of the eternal court of history will smile and tear to tatters the brief of the State Prosecutor and the sentence of this court. For she acquits us.

Hitler had, in fact, run away under gunfire, but no-one remembered that; he had scored a political triumph. He was sentenced to five years' imprisonment — an astonishingly light sentence for a convicted traitor, but the sort of sentence which was often given to right-wing extremists at this time, because the judges, who had mainly been appointed under the empire, did not in general like the republic and would pass heavy sentences only on socialists and liberals. Hitler, in fact, was to serve only a little more than one year of his sentence. From the jaws of defeat and humiliation he had managed, in a favourable situation, to snatch a sort of victory.

Mein Kampf — and Hitler's brand of Fascism

Hitler was in prison at Landsberg, where he was well treated — he put on a lot of weight in prison — and where, in the summer of

14 Hitler (left) and his followers (including Hess, second right), enjoy prison life in a Tyrolean mood.

1924, about forty other Nazis were in prison with him to whom he had constant access. The whole party spent many hours sitting outside wearing Bavarian leather shorts and Tyrolean jackets. When not doing this, Hitler spent much of his time dictating his one book, *Mein Kampf* (My Struggle), to his faithful follower, Hess. It is not a well-written book, but it is a most important record of the Nazi movement because it provides the best summary of Hitler's ideas which remained remarkably unchanging and rigid throughout his life. He puts his ideas forward with great honesty, so that it is a pity that few people, especially European statesmen, ever bothered to read the book, finding it full of turgid ramblings. If they had read it, they would have formed a clearer and more frightening picture of Hitler's intentions than they did when he came into power.

The book contains all Hitler's prejudices and hatreds — his extreme nationalism, his hatred of communism, his racialism and hatred of Jews, and his belief that the strong should dominate the weak and that a *Führer* or leader was essential. As we have remarked, these ideas were not Hitler's alone: they are components of an ideology and political movement which became strong in Europe between the wars and which was called Fascism. At the centre of Fascism was a belief in national greatness and the unity of the national community, where people were bound together by strong leadership, mass enthusiasm and by the open use of violence and brutality. Both Hitler and the Italian dictator who was to help him fight the Second World War, Benito Mussolini, can be described as Fascist leaders.

But the type of Fascism which Hitler and the Nazis developed was also unusual in many ways, shaped by Germany's particular situation in the middle of Europe and by her being potentially the most powerful nation of the continent. This partly explains Hitler's emphasis in the book on *Lebensraum* (living space). Hitler's theory was that the Germans were the leading branch of the North European master race, the Aryan or Nordic race. Because of their superiority, he believed, they were entitled to expand their living-space at the expense of inferior nations or races: this was biologically natural and necessary. By inferior races, Hitler meant the Slavs and Jews who lived in eastern Europe, and his conquest plans were largely at the expense of Russia which had become a communist state only, Hitler claimed, by a Jewish plot. He makes his plan of waging war on Russia quite plain in the book:

> And so we National Socialists consciously draw a line beneath the foreign policy tendency of our pre-war period . . . . We stop the endless German movement to the south and west, and turn our gaze towards the land in the east. At long last we break off the colonial and commercial policy of the pre-war period and shift to the soil policy of the future.

The German governments had been expansionist and nationalistic for some time, but the idea of fighting a war of extermination in the east, to win living-space on racial grounds, was specifically a Nazi idea and was to lead to frightful consequences for Europe. Hitler's schemes for empire were eventually to go wider and he was to declare war on the United States in 1941 in what can only have been a bid for world domination, but a racial empire in Europe was always to remain his chief goal. He also believed that Germany must defeat her traditional enemy, France, and he had colonial ambitions, but racial empire was the crux of the matter.

With its emphasis on biology, Nazi racism was much more extreme than that of other Fascist movements which, as in the Italian case, had small racialist elements. The Slavs were seen by Hitler as being only fit to work for the Germans; but the Jews were viewed

15 Hitler, as a prisoner in Landsberg, dreams of the world to conquer beyond the bars.

28

as non-human, parasites in all areas, working within both capitalism and communism in a fantastic plot. *Mein Kampf* is full of diatribes against them and in one passage Hitler even hints at the "final solution" of mass extermination, saying that the Jews had deserved to be held under poison gas for sabotaging the German war effort (in spite of the fact that as many Jews were fighting at the front as anyone else).

The book covers the more generally Fascist ideas: the need for the absolute leader and the national community. In Germany's case this was the joyful union of all the racially pure Aryans against their sub-human or non-human inferiors:

> The state of the folk . . . must set race in the centre of all life. It must take care to keep it pure . . . . It must see to it that only the healthy beget children . . .

This crude, destructive philosophy represented the genuine idea-system of Adolf Hitler. Of course, in some ways, it was only an attempt to justify intellectually a crude will to gain power and domination. Many of the Nazi leaders, like the cynical aristocrat Göring, probably only used these ideas to cover up their own desire to live off the fat of the land. Others, like Heinrich Himmler, the bespectacled leader of the SS, the Nazi terror organization, who looked like a typical middle-class German and became a murderer of millions, seem to have taken the Nazi world-view with utmost seriousness. And others, like Josef Goebbels who became Minister of Propaganda, were excited by the ideas of mass control and domination of the people. All of them, however, had committed themselves, for whatever reason, to an ideology which could lead only to cruelty and destruction and in which the perverted will of one man, Adolf Hitler, had power to decide the fate of millions.

The years of preparation

Hitler emerged from prison five days before Christmas 1924. During his imprisonment he had been careful to sow quarrels between the other party leaders so as to prevent their building up the party without him: he was determined to remain undisputed leader. He was to find, however, that the times had become less suitable for his movement. The economic crisis seemed to have largely passed and, under the guidance of her wise foreign minister, Gustav Stresemann, Germany seemed to be genuinely intent on reaching a lasting settlement with her European neighbours. Hitler again showed his skill during this unpromising period, which lasted a full five years, by building up the party organization, fighting cunning campaigns, scotching challenges to his leadership and preparing for better days. At the same time, for the last time in his life, he was able to indulge the taste of his youth for idleness and drifting. He would often speak of those times nostalgically:

> I used to spend the day in leather shorts. In the evening I would put on a dinner jacket or tails to go to the opera. We made excursions by car into the Fichtelgebirge and the Franconian mountains . . . . My super-charged Mercedes was a joy to all . . . . From all points of view, those were marvellous days.

The crisis of the Weimar Republic

In October 1929 the New York stock exchange crashed, millions lost all their savings and an economic depression on a scale unheard-of before began to spread around the world; this signalled the end of the "good years" of the Weimar Republic and would result in four years time in the coming to power of Hitler and the Nazis. Hitler had seen to it that the party was prepared.

The Nazis first won prominence in national politics in the later part of 1929. The conservative party, led by a businessman called

16   Hitler harangues an election crowd.

Alfred Hugenberg, were then campaigning against the Young Plan, the current effort to settle the differences between Germany and the other powers of Europe. They co-opted the Nazis into the campaign and this brought them national significance. It was the beginning of a pattern in which the other parties failed to take seriously the threat of Nazism, until it was too late. As the depression worsened and unemployment began to grow, elections were held in September 1930. The strident propaganda of the Nazis had a great effect in a situation of widespread resentment and many people seemed willing to believe that Jews and socialists were responsible for all Germany's troubles. The Nazis gained 107 seats in the German parliament or Reichstag and shot up to being the second largest party in Germany. This was in spite of the fact that Hitler made no secret of his plans to establish a dictatorship in Germany:

> It is not parliamentary majorities that mould the fate of nations. We know, however, that in this election democracy must be defeated with the weapons of democracy.

Hitler was equally frank in telling other politicians about the harsh fate he had in store for them, and yet they now began to think how they could reach an accommodation with him and offer him a share in power. In England the newspaper magnate, Lord Rothemere, extolled Hitler as being a bulwark against communism.

As the depression grew in severity, the Nazi vote grew by leaps and bounds. The message of national revival, public works programmes, revenge against the enemies who were making Germany pay large fines, and the identification of the Jews as scapegoats for every problem, seemed to have a lot to offer in a situation where there were six million unemployed. The open violence and terrorism of the movement did not so much repel people as persuade them that the Nazis meant business. By July 1932 the Nazis had 37 per cent of the voters, but were still short of the majority they needed if they were to come into power by popular vote. In November 1932, when more elections were held, the economic problems seemed at last to be lessening and the Nazi vote went down to 32 per cent. It began to seem as if the Nazis could only flourish in an atmosphere of crisis. After the July election, Sir Horace Rumbold, the perceptive British Ambassador in Berlin, had written home to his government:

> Hitler seems now to have exhausted his reserves. He has swallowed up the small bourgeois parties of the Middle and the Right, and there is no indication that he will be able to effect a breach in the centre, communist or socialist parties . . . . All the other parties are naturally gratified by Hitler's failure to reach anything like a majority on that occasion, especially as they are convinced that he has now reached his zenith.

As it turned out, they were too complacent — or in some cases, as we shall see, they fatally underestimated their man.

Hitler comes into power

At this period many conservative German politicians had finally lost whatever faith they had ever had in German democracy. They thought that a strongly authoritarian government would be the best answer and, seeing that Hitler had the biggest vote among the right-wing parties, they contemplated offering him a share in government, believing that they could easily tame his movement when in office. The French Military Attaché in Berlin, Colonel Chapouilly, summed up the views of General von Schleicher who was the last Chancellor (Prime Minister) before Hitler:

> In Schleicher's view, Hitler knows very well how to distinguish between the

17 In his newly found confidence as Chancellor, and backed by Göring in the chair, Hitler addresses the attentive-looking Reichstag in 1933.

demagogy suitable to a young Party, and the needs of national and international life. He has already moderated the actions of his troops on more than one occasion and one can secure more from him. Faced with the forces he controls, there is only one policy to adopt – to use him and win him over . . .

One of Hitler's greatest political assets throughout his life was the refusal of many of his opponents to take him seriously. People found it difficult to believe that a man who looked, as someone once said, like a shady beach-photographer, could be a terrible threat. The right-wing politicians conspired with Hitler at this period, the politicians of the middle would not unite against him, and the communists, only weeks before the Nazis came into power, co-operated with them in a Berlin tram-strike.

Hitler finally came into power by a sort of backstairs intrigue. The Weimar constitution gave great power to the President who at this

time was an aged aristocrat and General, Paul von Hindenburg. He had the power to choose the Chancellor who did most of the actual governing. A circle of aristocrats, generals and civil servants around Hindenburg were urging him to take Hitler on as Chancellor. This stiff-necked aristocrat was somewhat contemptuous of the former inhabitant of the Vienna doss-house, Hitler. Could such a man really be trusted to lead Germany? He offered Hitler a minor post in the government, but Hitler held out for the ultimate prize of the Chancellorship. And Hindenburg was an old man who could not stand out against constant urging. In January 1933 Hitler was appointed Chancellor in a government that had a majority of conservative and only three Nazi ministers. The conservatives were sure that they could keep effective power from the hands of the Nazis. Hindenburg, for his part, remained confused; on seeing the Nazi victory parades in the streets he is said to have murmured that he did not know that the German army had taken so many Russian prisoners.

The Nazis, however, now proceeded to take over control of the state from within, instituting purges of the police and civil service, ridding them of all people unsympathetic to the Nazi cause. On the night of 28 February 1933 the Reichstag (Parliament) building went up in flames. It seems that a crazy Dutchman, van der Lubbe, was responsible for the fire, but the Nazis, who now wanted an opportunity to tighten their grip on the country, treated the fire as a communist plot and declared a state of emergency, arresting and killing hundreds of people. It is possible, even, that the Nazis themselves started the fire and, in later years, Hitler was to make no secret of how he had cunningly used the fire for its news value:

18 Hitler and Hindenburg pose together in 1933 as joint guardians of German youth. Such a boy would later have been eligible to fight and die on the bloody Russian front.

During the Reichstag Fire I went in the middle of the night to the offices of the *Völkischer Beobachter*. It took half an hour before I could find anyone to let me in. Inside there were a few compositors sitting around, and eventually some sub-editor appeared heavy with sleep . . . . "There's no one here at this time of night; I must ask you to come back during business hours." "Are you mad!" I cried. "Don't you realize that an event of incalculable importance is actually now taking place?" In the end I got hold of Goebbels, and we worked till dawn preparing the next day's edition.

Hitler was obviously much more worried about a good story than any supposed communist plot. But the affair was made an excuse for suppressing and imprisoning communists and, in an atmosphere of violence and terror, the Nazis called new elections, hopefully to finally give them the majority they wanted to take dictatorial power by legal means. However, the voters stuck remarkably firm to their parties: the Nazi vote was just 44 per cent.

This was not to prove an insuperable obstacle, though. The Nazis were already in virtual control and they decided that the Reichstag could be persuaded to vote itself out of existence. The communists were already mostly in hiding and all other parties apart from the social democrats were willing to vote for the measure. By a large majority the Reichstag decided in March 1933 to terminate its own powers. More measures to control all independent organizations and to set up concentration camps to deal with opposition were already under way — Hitler did not need the legal process any more, but at least the fiction could be preserved that the Nazis had won power by the will of the people. In his diary on the night the Reichstag voted, Goebbels, the Nazi Minister of Propaganda wrote triumphantly: "Now are we also constitutionally the masters of the state".

Chapter Three 1933-1939

Hitler, the Peacetime Leader

Hitler, the German people and Nazism

When the Nazis came into power in Germany in 1933, they almost immediately imposed on the country one of the most thorough-going dictatorial regimes that the world has ever seen. It is known as the Third Reich.

All independent bodies within the state were crushed and a wide-ranging system of terror and control was set up so that the ordinary

19   A German girl, watched anxiously by her proud mother, receives the autograph book which the Führer has just signed for her.

20 Hitler, riding like an emperor, accepts the plaudits of the crowd at the Nürnberg rally of 1938.

citizen became scared of dropping even an idle word that could be interpreted as criticism of the regime. A great cult of Hitler's personality was set up, he was treated almost as a divine saviour, and the people were meant to be bound up in a mystical communion with him in which devotion to his will was seen as the highest satisfaction in life. All this was part of what was called the Nazi *Weltanschauung* (world-outlook). When the dream was shattered, the Germans were to see that this leader had brought them only destruction. But there can be no doubting that in the early years of his rule there was immense popular enthusiasm for him. No effort was spared to build up the cult of his personality. This is how his propaganda

20 Hitler, riding like an emperor, accepts the plaudits of the crowd at the Nürnberg rally of 1938.

Minister, Goebbels, spoke of him:

> he is like a child, kind, good, merciful. Like a cat: cunning, clever, agile. Like a lion: roaring, great and gigantic. A great guy, a man!

The party organized huge rallies, often held in the monumental new stadium and buildings at Nürnberg, where Hitler spoke amid scenes of incredible mass enthusiasm. Here is a description by an American foreign correspondent of the impact Hitler had when he entered the city in 1934:

> Like a Roman emperor Hitler rode into

this medieval town at sundown today past solid phalanxes of wildly cheering Nazis who packed the narrow streets . . . . About ten o'clock tonight I got caught in the mob of the thousand hysterics who jammed the moat in front of Hitler's hotel shouting: "We want our Führer". I was a little shocked at the faces, especially those of the women. They looked up at him as if he were a Messiah, their faces transformed . . .

It was common for women not to wash a hand for months that had touched the Führer. When he got to the rallies, with the crowds already wildly excited, Hitler would deliver magnetic speeches in which, in the later 1930s, he would utter terrible threats of vengeance against Germany's enemies. Hitler was one of the greatest orators in history; his voice was not beautiful, rather harsh and grating in fact, but he could understand the public mood instinctively and play on its hopes and fears. One of his most bitter critics, Otto Strasser, wrote like this of his oratory:

Hitler responds to the vibrations of the human heart with the delicacy of a seismograph, or perhaps of a wireless receiving set, enabling him . . . to act as a loudspeaker proclaiming the most secret desires, the least admissible instincts, the sufferings and personal revolts of a whole nation . . . . Adolf Hitler enters a hall. He sniffs the air. For a moment he gropes, feels his way, senses the atmosphere. Suddenly he bursts forth. His words go like an arrow to their target, he touches each private wound on the raw, liberating the mass unconscious, expressing its innermost aspirations, telling it what it most wants to hear.

The propaganda put forward by Nazism was that the whole nation was now united and moving forward to victory, creating prosperity at home and a more just situation regarding

21 Hitler addresses a massed crowd. Thousands stand to listen to the Führer's words.

Germany's neighbours abroad. How did this tally with the reality of Nazi rule? And how far was Hitler totally in control, as the propaganda said? It is true that Nazism did achieve remarkable successes in ending unemployment and restoring some prosperity to the country. But the Nazis had luck too, because they came into power when the depression was becoming less severe. Many of the jobs created were in building the magnificent road-system which still serves Germany well today. But others were in building expensive armaments for the purpose of fighting a destructive war or were created by forcing women to give up their jobs — according to the Nazis the woman's place was firmly in the home. The ordinary standard of living did not go up much although the state provided holidays and community activities which did something to compensate for any hardship.

In the early days, if you did nothing that the regime did not like, you were safe from the concentration camp. Distinguished artists and scientists went into exile and this was an immense impoverishment of German cultural life. Some other artists and intellectuals, although not many, tried to find some means of protest while remaining in Germany. In 1933 Ricarda Huch, the distinguished historian and novelist, resigned from the Prussian Academy of Arts rather than consent to the expulsion of certain other members. In her letter of resignation she wrote:

That a German should feel German I should take almost for granted. But there are different opinions about what is German and how German-ness is to be expressed. What the present regime prescribes as national sentiment is not my German-ness. The centralization, the compulsion, the brutal methods, the defamation of people who think differently, the boastful self-praise I regard as un-German and unhealthy. Possessing a philosophy that varies so radically from that prescribed

39

by the state I find it impossible to remain one of its academicians.

Many newspapers which were liberal or had Jewish owners, were forced to close down, but the ordinary citizen did not care much about this.

Measures of persecution against the Jews began almost immediately with a boycott of Jewish shops, but the ordinary German could ignore the mounting wave of terror against his Jewish neighbours, while industrialists found that the pickings from confiscated Jewish firms and the abolition of trade unions did much to compensate for Nazi control and directives and to justify the support that some of them had given to the regime at the start. In the peacetime years the Germans were content and terror did

22 Hitler opens a new Autobahn with great pomp and ceremony.

23 Hitler next to Hess with a group of old Nazis enjoys Bavarian mountain life. The cares of state are obviously not weighing heavily on the Nazis at this moment!

not matter much. In the dreadful night of plunder and murder against the Jews in November 1938 — called "Crystal Night" because of all the smashed glass — a German woman saw a piano belonging to a cultured Jew being thrown from a window by Nazi thugs. She merely remarked mildly that a piano could hardly help who it belonged to.

How far was this system the direct result of Hitler's work? The first point to make is that, until the war years at least, Hitler never entirely lost the Bohemian drifting habits of his youth: he was a lazy ruler whose day began at twelve and often he spent the afternoons in Munich tea-shops eating cakes and talking interminably. Obviously he alone

41

could not personally carry out the government of a complex modern state. Some matters — the development of foreign policy, for instance, or the growing campaign against the Jews — were personal interests and all major decisions were made by Hitler in person. But below this the Nazi regime was a mass of little competing empires run by the other Nazi leaders. The Nazis had an impressive word — *Gleichschaltung* (Co-ordination) — for bringing previously independent bodies such as trade unions, youth groups, farmers' unions and the like under Nazi control. The aim was to create a totalitarian state, a state where total control was achieved over people's lives, and this *was* achieved in part. But very

24 Hitler and Hess on the balcony inspect the Hitler Youth as they march past at a Nürnberg rally.

often the reality was that some Nazi bigwig was given a little area of life to control and exploit: there was corruption and some inefficiency. Hitler's method of ruling was to play the minor leaders off against each other to ensure his continued total final control, but they were all so much in awe of his personality anyway that perhaps he need not have bothered. Speer, one of the more independent of them, says this:

They were all under his spell, blindly obedient to him and with no will of their own — whatever the medical term for this phenomenon may be I noticed, during my activities as architect, that to be in his presence for any length of time, made me feel exhausted and *void*. Capacity for independent work was paralysed.

There was only one major attempt to dispute Hitler's rule during the first ten years of what was called the Third Reich. This was in 1934 and concerned Ernst Röhm who was the leader of the Nazi private army, the SA. Röhm represented the original radical and even socialist aims of the party; he wanted to turn the SA into a people's army to supplant the official German army which was run by aristocrats. But Hitler was much more interested in foreign conquest, for which he needed the traditional army, than in any social reforms. Röhm was an old personal friend of Hitler's but when it seemed that his power might offer a challenge to Hitler, the dictator acted swiftly and ruthlessly. Röhm and the other major SA leaders were shot and a general bloodbath was set in train to remove anyone who, for whatever reason, Hitler felt might be a threat. Gisevius, later one of the 1944 conspirators against Hitler, describes the scene at the Berlin airport when Hitler came back from Munich having had Röhm executed in "The Night of the Long Knives":

A brown shirt, black bow-tie, dark-brown leather jacket, high black army boots.
He wore no hat; his face was pale, unshaven, sleepless, at once gaunt and puffed. Under the forelock pasted against his forehead his eyes stared dully . . . . From one of his pockets Himmler took a long tattered list. Hitler read it through while Göring and Himmler whispered incessantly into his ear. Now and then he paused for a moment at one of the names . . . . The bathos of the scene, the woebegone expression, the combination of violent fantasy and grim reality, the gratuitously blood-red sky like a scene out of Wagner — it was really too much for me.

Himmler, the SS leader, was to take over most of the SA functions and in his organization was to develop such an effective reign of terror that resistance to Hitler's rule became virtually impossible. Shortly after this scene in 1934 the old president, Hindenburg, died and Hitler took the office of President for himself: no-one was to be able to dispute his power again. It was only when the regime was staring defeat in the face that any revolt against it would begin again.

The bloodbath of "The Night of the Long Knives" also passed without public comment. As Hitler's increasingly ruthless foreign policy led ever more quickly to war, people began to have their doubts. They wanted order and discipline; they did not want war. But most comment, both German and foreign, remained favourable; the tales of Jewish refugees arriving in other countries, stripped of all their belongings, went unheeded. In Germany there was the occasional sceptical comment; the writer Oswald Spengler, reflecting on the corruption of Nazi rule, remarked sarcastically that Nazi policy was "the organization of those who can't find work by those who won't do any", but this was an isolated comment. Until war came the Germans were content and Hitler could even seem, in spite of some of the evidence, to be a successful ruler: at home there was order, he had gained territory abroad and made Germany's name feared. The historian, Joachim Fest, reflects on what would be Hitler's reputation now if he had died in 1938 before disaster set in:

few would hesitate to call him one of the greatest of German statesmen, the consummator of Germany's history. The aggressive speeches and *Mein Kampf*, the anti-Semitism and the design for world domination, would presumably have fallen into oblivion, dismissed as the man's youthful fantasies, and only occasionally would critics remind an irritated nation

25 Hitler marches in front of Röhm, the subordinate he is shortly to murder, at an SA rally in Kiel. Röhm and his companions wear the brown SA uniform that had become a symbol of torture and violence in Germany.

of them. Six-and-one-half years separated Hitler from such renown. Granted, only premature death could have given him that, for by nature he was headed towards destruction and did not make an exception of himself. Can we call him great?

26　Hitler at a motor show acts the role of responsible peacetime leader in 1939. Goebbels is first left, Göring second left.

The false peace

For the first four years of his rule from 1933 to 1937 Hitler was relatively quiet in his foreign policy, making only one major aggressive move in Europe. Then in the next two years the pace of aggression quickened, several major countries became victims, and war came in 1939.

The major reason for Hitler's relative caution in the early days was that he did not feel that the time was yet ripe for foreign conquest. Germany's army and economy were still weak and the country was hemmed in by a network of treaties which had been signed to uphold the situation created by the Versailles peace treaty of 1919. These treaties had been formed mainly by Germany's traditional enemy, France, with the aim of countering any possible German aggression. Therefore, one of Hitler's first acts was to conclude a non-aggression treaty in 1934 with Poland, a country which he was later ruthlessly to attack. He also signed a naval agreement with Britain in 1935. His ability to wait and to choose the correct psychological moment was one of Hitler's greatest political gifts. He told Rauschning at this time:

No matter what you attempt if an idea is not yet mature you will not be able to realize it. Then there is only one thing to do: have patience, wait, try again, wait again. In the subconscious, the work goes on. It matures, sometimes it dies. Unless I have the inner, incorruptible conviction: *this is the solution*, I do nothing. Not even if the whole party tries to drive me into action.

At the same time we must admit that, from the start, foreign statesmen were foolish if they did not realize where Hitler's policies could lead. He never ceased to fulminate against the Treaty of Versailles, he withdrew from the League of Nations in 1933 and he began hasty re-armament in Germany from almost the start of his rule. As he himself said in a speech in 1941:

> My programme was to abolish the Treaty of Versailles. It is nonsense for the rest of the world to pretend otherwise today that I did not reveal this programme until 1933, or 1935, or 1937. Instead of listening to the foolish chatter of emigrés, these gentlemen would have been better advised to read what I have written and rewritten thousands of times.

As we now know, Hitler's programme was much wider than a revision of the treaty: it involved an immense expansion of Germany's frontiers. But the warning was clear. The belief, which many western statesmen held, that Hitler could be made reasonable by granting some of his demands — the belief which historians call "appeasement" — was based on a fundamental lack of understanding of the character of a ruthless dictator.

Hitler's one major aggressive move during those first four years was to march into the Rhineland in March 1936. This area had formerly been a part of Germany but had been declared a demilitarized zone (an area cleared of military installations) because it was an essential buffer zone against German attack on France. To occupy it, therefore, was to risk provoking the western powers,

Britain and France, and if they had been ready to fight at the time there could have been war. Hitler made this risky move in 1936 because he now felt stronger and also he was drawing closer to the Fascist regime in Italy which had recently been conducting an aggressive war against Abyssinia without interference from Britain or France. Even so, Germany was not really ready to fight at this point. Hitler's move was a gamble which paid off: once again, the western powers let the incident pass without comment. Hitler was jubilant at the success of his psychological understanding of his opponents:

> What would have happened if anybody other than myself had been at the head of the Reich! Anybody you care to name would have lost his nerve. I was obliged to lie and what saved me was my unshakeable obstinacy and my amazing aplomb. I threatened unless the situation eased to send six extra divisions into the Rhineland. The truth was I only had four brigades. Next day the English papers wrote that there had been an easing of the situation.

These were crude bullying tactics, but for the time being they worked.

The attack on Austria

From about 1937 Hitler began to plan war in the near future. In 1936 a "Rome-Berlin Axis" was formed between the Italian and the German dictatorships: at the same time both powers were growing closer to the militaristic rulers in Japan whose plans for a great empire in Asia bore some similarity to Hitler's plans for Europe. Rearmament was going on in Germany now at a very rapid pace. Hitler may also have been influenced by personal considerations: he was almost fifty now, failing in health, and felt that no-one but himself could be trusted to build the great German

27 Lloyd George, a western statesman, was impressed by Hitler when he went to visit him in 1936.

empire. He was not entirely sure when he wanted war; he would let circumstances decide for him. He said to Ciano, the Italian foreign minister, in October 1936:

> German and Italian rearmament is proceeding much more rapidly than rearmament in Great Britain, where it is not only a case of producing ships, guns and aeroplanes, but also of undertaking psychological rearmament, which is much longer and more difficult. In three years Germany will be ready, in four years more than ready; if five years are given better still . . .

At the Hossbach Conference, called in November 1937, Hitler declared that he was planning war before about 1943. He outlined some of his plans for empire and indicated the first two nations to be attacked: Austria and Czechoslovakia. It was a characteristic of Hitler's conduct of policy that, though his aims were fixed, he was quite flexible about his timing and methods. He still hoped to avoid war with Britain; he could not be quite certain if Italy would fight with him. But he was certain that he had a mission which he would be able to accomplish. He once said:

> I go the way that providence directs with the confidence of a sleepwalker.

The first nation to be taken over, Hitler had decided, was to be Austria. He himself had been born an Austrian (he had taken out German citizenship as late as 1932) and in his youth he had fiercely hated the multi-racial Austro-Hungarian empire. Since the Treaty of Versailles settlement the country had been an independent republic, but many Austrians, although not all, wanted union with the German Reich. Hitler first made sure that Mussolini, the Italian dictator, would be willing for him to take over a country which was on Italy's borders. Then in February 1938 he summoned the Austrian ruler, Schuschnigg, a dictator who ruled with the support of the Roman Catholic Church, to meet him at his Bavarian home in the moun-

tains, the Berghof. Hitler bullied the unfortunate ruler into appointing a pro-Nazi government in Austria, telling him that no other country would lift a finger to save Austria from German invasion and even abusing Schuschnigg for having had defence works built on the Austrian frontier:

> Listen. You don't really think that you can move a single stone in Austria without my hearing about it, do you? You don't seriously believe that you can stop me, or even delay me for half an hour, do you? . . . After that the Army, the SA, and the Austrian Legion would move in, and nobody can stop their just revenge — not even I.

These tactics were successful in getting the Austrian ruler to accept the new government, but then in early March came the news that Schuschnigg was planning to hold a plebiscite (public vote on a particular issue) to ask the Austrians whether they wanted to join Germany; it seemed likely that the majority would vote against. Hitler acted swiftly. On the night of 10-11 March German forces moved into Austria and swiftly took over the country. To Hitler it was the fulfilment of the first stage of a dream:

> I believe that it was God's will to send a youth from here into the Reich, to let him grow up, to raise him to be the leader of the nation so as to enable him to lead back his homeland into the Reich . . .

Hitler told the press: "For me this is the proudest hour of my life".

The reality was rather different. The Nazis followed up their success in taking over Austria by immediately building a concentration camp and the Austrians soon grew resentful under German exploitation. There took place, too, the most horrific persecutions of Jews that had yet taken place; old Jewish men were forced to get down on all fours to clean pavements and a wave of suicides followed this systematic campaign of brutality. Europe began to learn what it could expect from Nazi rule.

The rape of Czechoslovakia

The next attack — on Czechoslovakia — now followed within months. The Czechs were a Slavic people and therefore branded by Hitler as racial inferiors; he had always had a special hatred for them. But their state was strong and the only democracy in eastern Europe. However, in one corner of the country, the Sudetenland, which was a vital buffer zone against German attack, there lived a German population. These people had real grievances against the Czech government, which Hitler was able to use as a lever to start off his attack on Czechoslovakia. In this way his conduct appeared reasonable. Hitler instructed the Germans in the Sudetenland to press ever more violent demands for their rights and eventually for independence; and indeed, by April 1938, they were demanding an autonomous state. Hitler's final aim was the destruction of the whole Czech state, but this was a good start. Throughout the summer of 1938 tension mounted. The western powers, Britain and France, who in spite of the evidence still believed in the policy of "appeasement", were not inclined to risk a world war over Czechoslovakia. The British Prime Minister, Neville Chamberlain, a sincere, rather naïve man who genuinely believed in "appeasement", called it a "far-away country of which we know nothing" and in September 1938 he made several trips to Germany to see Hitler and try to reach a peaceful solution with him. Hitler knew exactly how to play on Chamberlain's nerves:

> All this seems to be academic; I want to get down to realities. Three hundred Sudetens have been killed, and things of that kind cannot go on; the thing has got to be settled at once. I am determined to settle it; I do not care whether there is a world war or not. I am determined

to settle it and to settle it soon; I am prepared to risk a world war rather than allow this to drag on.

Perhaps Chamberlain really believed that Hitler had been roused to such threats by the deaths of three hundred Sudeten Germans in the disturbances; more certainly he was genuinely horrified, as Hitler was not, by the idea of a world war. A conference finally met at Munich at the end of September 1938 to settle the problem — Hitler, Mussolini, Chamberlain and the French Premier, Daladier were there; the Czechs were not invited but representatives waited outside the conference room to learn their fate. They were forced to give up the Sudetenland, a large part of their military capacity, and more territory to Hungary and Poland, and they had to accept a new pro-German government.

After this the final collapse of Czechoslovakia was only a matter of time; Hitler continued to foment disturbances there. In March 1939 he summoned Hachà, the aged Czech President, and bullied him so much that he fainted; when he recovered consciousness there was a paper waiting for him to sign asking the Germans to come in and "protect" the Czechs. The German army moved in and the familiar pattern of terror and exploitation began.

The coming of Hitler's war

Hitler's next victim was Poland. Once again his aim was the total destruction of the state and once again there was a genuine grievance which he could use as a lever to start off his attack. Under the Treaty of Versailles, a stretch of land called the "Polish Corridor" had been taken from Germany to give the new state of Poland access to the sea. Hitler now demanded the return of this land. But Europe was by this time beginning to understand Hitler. To his surprise, the Poles stood firm in reply to his demands; equally surprisingly the British government, soon after Hitler's triumphal entry into the Czech capital, Prague, declared themselves willing to defend Poland if she were attacked. Hitler was not worried; he did not really believe that Britain would fight him or that the Poles would be able to resist him. He had wanted his war a little later, but he was prepared to have it now.

Hitler, in fact, had everything to gain from waiting a year or two for suspicions to lull, but his political weaknesses were now beginning to show themselves. Power had gone to his head and he did not know where to stop. The risk did not seem too great; his alliance with Mussolini was now close and he had been testing his new fighter

planes in the recent Spanish Civil War, helping the side of the nationalists and Fascists and bombing whole villages like Guernica where more than six hundred people were killed. In May 1939 he told his generals that war was now inevitable:

> Further successes can no longer be attained
> without the shedding of blood . . . . It is
> a question of expanding our living-space in
> the east, of securing our food-supplies,
> and of settling the Baltic problem . . . .
> There is no question of sparing Poland
> and we are left with the decision: to attack
> Poland at the first suitable opportunity.

All that remained now before war could start was for the remaining great power of Europe to take sides — Russia, or the Soviet Union, which in 1917 had become the world's

28   Hitler visits his new territory of the Sudetenland in December 1938.

29 Hitler makes his presence felt as the new master of Czechoslovakia, in April 1939.

first communist state. Hitler had been heaping abuse on communism for years and his final aim was to conquer Russia, but this did not stop him from being quicker than Britain and France to reach an accommodation with the Soviet Union. In August 1939 the Nazi-Soviet Pact was signed; Hitler and the Soviet leader, Josef Stalin, agreed to carve up Poland between them.

On 1 September 1939 the German armies, on another jumped-up pretext, invaded Poland, soon to meet invading Russian armies from the east. Two days later Britain and France declared war on Germany. Hitler now had his war. His astonishing luck was to hold for a couple of years yet, but after that it was to run out for good.

Chapter Four

Hitler as Politician and Personality

Hitler the man

Hitler was an unusual political personality in many ways. He felt himself to be on an inspired mission, and that, guided by this mission, he had formed his movement. He had never had to work his way up within a movement, jostle for power with other politicians, or modify his ideas. These facts were reflected in the sort of leader he was. He had political gifts — but his whole personality was that of a highly neurotic individual, perhaps even a psychopath. There is no doubt that towards the end of his life, under the immense pressures of war, Hitler was clinically mad.

His personality seems deficient in many ways. He was absolutely rigid in his ideas and humourlessly furious when they were flouted. He was once corrected by a secretary on the tune of a song he was humming. He shouted:

> I don't have it wrong. It is the composer who made a mistake in this passage.

Hitler, in fact, was immensely concerned with his own dignity but many character traits, such as his total lack of a sense of the ridiculous, could make him appear foolish.

When he encountered open defiance, he could go into hysterical rages when he seemed almost to have lost his reason. When it looked as if England would go to war with Hitler in September 1939, a Swedish diplomat was astonished to witness the following scene:

> Hitler jumped up and became very agitated. He nervously paced up and down and declared, as if he were talking to himself, that Germany was invincible . . . . "If there is a war," he said, "I will build U-Boats, U-Boats, U-Boats!" His voice became increasingly indistinct and gradually one could no longer understand him. Suddenly he collected himself, raised his voice as if addressing a vast assembly and screamed, "I will build airplanes, airplanes, airplanes and I'll annihilate my enemies!" . . . I looked at him in amazement.

Hitler had something of the child who goes mad if he is flouted. All his life he retained the tastes of his suburban childhood — a love of chocolates and sugar, of picnics and films, of childish games like seeing who could spot the most men wearing beards — games which the Almighty Führer was always terribly disappointed not to win. He also had the cruelty that children often have; he wanted to have his enemies punished as

30 Hitler sometimes could not avoid looking ridiculous in moments of elation. This is a still from a film taken with a miniature movie camera by Eva Braun's sister.

harshly as possible. After the attempt on his life in July 1944 the leading conspirators were executed by hanging by piano-wire from meathooks fixed to the ceiling; an agonizing death. Hitler had a film made of their deaths for private viewing with his cronies; Speer, his Minister of Armaments, says that Hitler "loved the film and had it shown over and over again; it became one of his favourite entertainments".

Hitler did not think that such delighting in cruelty was wrong. He was obsessed, in fact, with the general need in life for cruelty and hardness, so much so that one cannot help suspecting that he had a massive inferiority complex and a need for compensation. His inflexibility, combined with his cruelty, meant that he did not care how many lives were lost through his actions. He said to Rauschning, first a Nazi but then in exile from Germany and a bitter critic of Nazism:

Nature is cruel, therefore we too must be cruel. If I can send the flower of the German nation into the hell of war, without the smallest pity for the spilling of precious German blood, then surely I have the right to remove millions of an inferior race that breeds like vermin.

By the "inferior race" Hitler meant the Jews. We notice in this passage that it did not seem to matter to Hitler who got killed, magnificent Germans or "vermin" Jews; their blood was equally to be spilled. This shows an immense lust for destruction on Hitler's part.

Hitler was full of his own ideas and expected them to be taken with utmost seriousness by all around. He hated smoking; no smoking was allowed in his presence. Guests who ate meat were subjected to long lectures at the meal on the virtues of vegetarianism. Hitler had views on all sorts of topics — he delivered endless tirades about the evil of the Catholic Church, diet recipes, Greek temples, police dogs, the supposed Mongoloid origin of the Czechs and all sorts of other subjects — and his weary servants and adjutants were forced to listen to these boring monologues far into the night because Hitler had insomnia. The mixture in Hitler's head of half-baked ideas, together with a great capacity for cruelty, meant that he was capable of taking the racial philosophy of the Nazi movement seriously and of using it to justify the deaths

31 Hitler and Eva Braun in the centre. Eva's former employer, the photographer, Hoffmann, is on the left. Hitler's quack doctor, Morell, is in the background.

of millions of innocent people.

Hitler's inhumanity as a politician was also owing to the fact that he was incapable of responding to individual people as individuals, and could only really build up a relationship as an impassioned speaker with a vast crowd. His life was bare of the satisfaction of friends, lovers or family. All the women with whom Hitler was most involved either attempted to commit suicide or did actually kill themselves. This was true of Angela Raubal, his niece and the one person with whom he ever seems truly to have been in love. She committed suicide in 1931 because the strain of her relationship with Hitler was becoming too much for her, exactly why we do not know. During the time that he was dictator, Hitler had a regular girlfriend, Evan Braun, who had been a photographer's model, but she was treated very coolly and was never allowed to appear with Hitler in public. Hitler in fact despised women as weak creatures; he once said to the wife of a minor Nazi leader:

> A woman must be a cute, cuddly, naïve little thing — tender, sweet and stupid.

Speer, the perceptive architect who became Hitler's Minister of Armaments, said of Eva Braun:

> She was pleasant and fresh-faced rather than beautiful and had a modest air . . . . Eva Braun kept her distance from every one of Hitler's intimates . . . . She was well aware of her dubious position in Hitler's court.

Eva herself, a childish and not very intelligent woman who only wanted Hitler's love, seems to have often been made miserable by the way she was neglected. In her diary for 1935 she wrote:

> I have happily reached the age of 23, though whether I'm happy is another question. Right now I'm anything but. If only I had a puppy, then I wouldn't be so lonely. But no doubt that is asking too much.

Eva was kept at the Berghof, the house that Hitler had had built in the Bavarian Alps, but as the years passed Hitler paid her less and less attention.

Just as Hitler's life was empty of the personal satisfaction of friendship, so it was also lacking in interests to make him a fuller person. He claimed to love music, but in reality he could only appreciate a few composers, especially Wagner whose operas based on old German myths seemed to fit in well with the Nazi *Weltanschauung*. He had a genuine passion for architecture — the frustrated passion of his youth — and spent hours poring over vast building plans with his young architect and later Minister of Armaments, Albert Speer. But Hitler was only really interested in architecture as a means of expressing Nazi power and, under the pressure of war, few of the buildings planned were ever constructed.

In his private life, Hitler was the typical lower-middle-class German, but one with a particularly empty life. Many people have remarked on what careful, old-fashioned manners he could have, but this politeness could turn all too easily to violence and terrifying anger, and it masked a total ruthlessness. In reality this personality had only one interest and only one satisfaction — power. This was to become ever truer with the passing years.

32 Hitler and Eva Braun take a walk together.

△
33 Hitler reads the papers over breakfast.

◁ 34 Hitler in animated mood on the telephone.

35 Hitler warms to his topic in the middle of a ▷
characteristic speech.

Hitler the politician

As we have said, Hitler was a lazy ruler; at the height of the political crisis in 1932 he and Dr Goebbels loved nothing better than to slip in to see the latest trash film. But this masked an astonishing ability of Hitler's to isolate problems and to attend with great concentration to the matters he felt were important. This method of working suited him because he had a vision of himself as an artist, a man with a mission. But his greatest political gift was undoubtedly his psychological understanding, both of the people he ruled — he really convinced the Germans, for instance, that he was simply someone who

represented them and their justified desires — and of foreign politicians, whom he knew how to bully and persuade. Allied to this was his magnificent sense of timing — his ability to wait for the right moment. Time and time again in the early 1930s, for example, he was offered a share in power, but under great pressure he always stood out for the greatest prize of the Chancellorship.

Moreover, although some of his enemies tried to present Hitler as a totally ignorant and incompetent man, this is by no means true. He had a great deal of knowledge of all sorts of important matters concerning his policies. Grand Admiral Dönitz, the naval chief, declared in 1967:

> Naval officers who have spent some time with Hitler . . . have told me that he was an expert on all the ships listed in Meyer's Naval Pocket Book. Because of his excellent memory he was better informed about their displacement, guns and armour than . . . many sailors in his entourage.

When war came, Hitler was to show himself able to take command of the fighting in

many ways; many campaigns were to be won because his sense of strategy was more daring than those of the German generals. Where he failed, though, was in the overall planning of the war and in his idea of what could actually be achieved on the field of battle; his rigidity of mind and his growing fanaticism were to blame for this.

Hitler was, in fact, a strange mixture of rigidity and flexibility. As we have seen, he had a great gift for adapting his plans to suit changing circumstances. He was absolutely rigid in his contempt for institutions like the Christian Churches, with their Gospel that condemned selfishness and praised self-sacrifice — not a philosophy that appealed to Hitler. And yet he was cynically prepared to work with them if they presented no challenges to his rule. But in his basic plans and his few simple, crude ideas Hitler never faltered. By the end of the war he had become a mad fanatic with two simple over-riding aims: to knock out his enemies with as much force as possible and to exterminate the European Jews. This was not the mind of a constructive politician. Even so, he had established an authority over the German politicians and people so great that only his suicide and the collapse of his empire were to break it. Only then were the Germans to realize what an evil spell they had been under.

The urge towards destruction

We have painted a picture of Hitler as man and politician with grave faults. But perhaps his greatest fault, which his movement also expressed, was a total indifference to human values. Nazism was the first political philosophy for centuries to believe that violence and brutality are justified for their own sakes:

> I must be a harsh master . . . we must be ruthless . . . . We are barbarians! We want to be barbarians! It is an honourable title. We shall rejuvenate the world . . . . It is our mission to cause unrest.

This is no more than the exact truth about Hitler and his movement. What ensured that, in spite of his great gifts, Hitler could never be regarded as a great leader was his total inability to make plans that would benefit anyone, which in turn sprang from his inability as a human being to love anyone. Destruction was his only real aim and his only achievement. At the end of his life, when Germany lay in ruins, he believed only that there should be more destruction; nothing should be allowed to survive his death. It is doubtful if he ever even cared for the Germans whom he had tried to persuade that they were the master race; he thought of them only as an army which would carry out his plans and be subordinate to his will. There was only one choice: success or death. In 1942, speaking to his associates and when the tide was turning against him, he anticipated in his thoughts his own death and the destruction of his people:

> In short, if one hadn't a family to bequeath one's house to, the best thing would be to burn it with all its contents — a magnificent funeral pyre!

36 Hitler practises throwing hand-grenades as a spare-time hobby.

Chapter Five 1939-1945

Hitler as Warlord

Hitler's war?

The Second World War, which lasted for six years from 1939 to 1945 and in which thirty million Europeans died, has become known as Hitler's War. Is this a good description? It was much more complex than that, of course; during the six years a majority of the world's countries became involved in the conflict, and a great variety of different conflicts — the Chinese civil war, the Japanese-Chinese War, the Japanese-American war in the Pacific, the Greek Civil War and many others — all became caught up in the same big war. It was a period of great turmoil which would have happened even without Hitler. But there can be no doubt that the explosive energies of the Nazi movement were what brought Europe to war in 1939, unwillingly on the part of the other nations, and that Hitler himself bears a heavy responsibility for planning and setting the war in motion. During the course of the war he was to urge his soldiers and agents on to ever more terrible acts of savagery and terror. The Second World War is justly called Hitler's War.

The conquest of Poland

Poland was overrun by German and Russian armies in just three weeks. The Poles fought bravely, but they were helpless against the new style of warfare, the *Blitzkrieg* (lightning war) which the German armies had developed, consisting of a merciless advance of quick-moving panzer tanks protected by low-flying planes. The two invading armies met and quickly partitioned the country between them. Russia, which had done scarcely any fighting, took half the land as a reward for her acquiescence in Hitler's schemes.

The Polish war was planned as a war of exploitation and extermination from the start. The Poles were Slavs who deserved no mercy. Before the war started Hitler had given directions to his generals:

> Close your hearts to pity. Act brutally. Eighty million people must obtain what is their right. Their existence must be made secure. The strongest man is right. The greatest harshness.

In this spirit the Polish war was fought. Hitler had determined to destroy the Polish governing class and anyone capable of defying German rule. He stated this very plainly: "The men capable of leadership in Poland must be liquidated". And by the end of 1941 100,000 clergy, nobles and intellectuals had been murdered. Hitler made it quite

37 Hitler in Warsaw lectures to German officers about the Polish campaign.

clear that treatment of the Poles should be brutal. He said:

> The Poles, in direct contrast to our German workmen, are especially born for hard labour . . . . It is necessary to keep the standard of life low in Poland. There should be one master only for the Poles — the Germans. Therefore the representatives of the intelligentsia are to be exterminated. This sounds cruel, but such is the law of life.

Poland was ruthlessly exploited for slave labourers; thousands were simply kidnapped off the streets and sent to toil in the Reich; many of these died owing to the appalling conditions they were subjected to. The advance into Poland had also been accompanied by a great deal of killing of any Jews who could be found; it was common to drive all the Jews in an area into a local synagogue and set it on fire. The treatment of Poland was a true blueprint for Europe under Hitler. But for Hitler it was just a stage on the onward march to Russia, at that moment his ally. His policy was to neglect Poland, leaving

it to grow wild, but he made exceptions of territories close to the Russian frontier. He told Keitel, one of his generals, in October 1939:

> The territory is important to us from a military point of view as an advanced jumping-off point and can be used for the strategic concentration of troops. To that end the railroads, roads and lines of communication are to be kept in order.

The Blitzkrieg in the west

But for the present Hitler's enemies were the western powers, Britain and France, and he wanted to knock them out before tackling Russia. The western powers, although they were at war, had made little attempt to help Poland, and the war in the west took a long time to get going — the English called it the "phoney war" and the Germans the "sitting war". Hitler kept on delaying his attack until what he felt was a suitable opportunity and both sides sat uneasily behind their fortifications until the spring of 1940.

In April 1940 Hitler launched an attack on Denmark and Norway which were speedily defeated, and one month later the main attack on the west began — on Belgium, Holland and France. It was another *Blitzkrieg* but even more devastating than the first. The Germans had launched a surprise attack through the Ardennes mountains which bypassed the French defences and struck right at the heart of France. It is possible that this may have been partly Hitler's own idea; certainly he believed that he ought to be the supreme military as well as political leader and was constantly overruling his generals. He was frightened by the possibility of a French counter-attack from the south. General Halder wrote in his diary for 18 May:

> Every hour is precious. Führer's H.Q. sees it very differently. Führer keeps worrying about south flank. He rages and screams that we are on the way to ruin a whole

campaign. He won't have any part in continuing the operation in a westward direction.

The generals resented Hitler's interference and secretly regarded him as an amateur, but in this campaign and in several others it seems probable that they owed much of their success to him. As the war went on he disregarded their advice more and more frequently and sacked them when they disagreed. Hardly a German general or Field-Marshal survived the whole war with the same job. By this time, however, Hitler's military instincts were more often bad than good.

On 17 June 1940 the French government asked Hitler for peace. This was a great moment for Hitler. The total defeat of France had long been a dream of German nationalists and now he, the unknown soldier of the first war, had accomplished this dream. For the signing of the armistice he chose the exact railway carriage in the Forest of Compiègne where the Germans had been forced to sign a capitulation in 1918. To him it seemed a magnificent gesture of revenge. An American correspondent, eavesdropping intently fifty yards away with field glasses, caught the scene:

> He swiftly snaps his hands on his hips, arches his shoulders, plants his feet wide apart. It is a magnificent gesture of defiance, of burning contempt for this place and all that it has stood for in the twenty-two years since it witnessed the humbling of the German Empire.

After a swift sightseeing tour of Paris, which he found inferior to Italian and German cities, Hitler returned to Berlin. His only remaining problem now was Britain. The Italian dictator, Mussolini, sensing that the war was won, had recently joined him in the fighting. Hitler fully expected that the British

38   Hitler in Paris combines the roles of conqueror and somewhat unimpressed tourist by the Eiffel Tower.

would now see reason; if they would allow him a free hand in Europe, they could keep their empire unharmed — for the time being, anyway. But the British had recently replaced the appeasing Chamberlain with the energetic war leader Winston Churchill and they soon made it clear that they would not come to terms with Germany. Hitler made a direct appeal to the British:

> In this hour I feel it to be my duty before my own conscience to appeal once more to reason and common sense in Great Britain as much as elsewhere. I consider myself in a position to make this appeal since I am not the vanquished begging favours, but the victor speaking in the name of reason. I can see no reason why this war must go on.

In truth, the British were taking a terrible risk in resisting Hitler. Their army had been largely destroyed in France (a remnant had escaped in small boats from the Dunkirk beaches at the end of May and beginning of June). Their armaments and number of planes did not match the German strength. And only the narrow channel, protected by the planes of the RAF flying over, could save them from the full force of the lightning war.

39 A battle over London, 6 September 1940.

Once the British had decided to resist him, Hitler made ruthless plans for establishing a rule of terror in Britain as soon as he had conquered it. But the British people had decided that Hitler was an international and human menace who must be destroyed at all costs. So their pilots prepared to defend the narrow channel crossing; if they failed to do this, their chances of resisting the German army would be small indeed.

This battle of the skies — the "Battle of Britain" — lasted from July to September 1940. The German fighter planes did not prove a match for the British ones and Hitler was not so intent on defeating Britain that he was prepared to lose his entire air force to do it — he needed it for his plans for the east. From September Hitler switched the attack to night-time bombing of major cities, especially London which now suffered a "blitz" that destroyed many of the beautiful buildings of the city and took many lives. On 12 October a brief directive was issued:

> The Führer has decided that from now on until the spring, preparations for Sea-Lion shall be continued solely for the purpose of maintaining political and military pressure on England.
> Should the invasion be reconsidered in the spring or early summer of 1941, orders for a renewal of operational readiness will be issued later . . .

It was Hitler's first defeat, and the invasion was never to be resumed. The British had fulfilled their aim of keeping the war going and staving off Hitler. Hitler's attention now

40 A bronze relief, showing the heads of Hitler and Mussolini, presented to the Führer on his 50th birthday, 1939.

turned back to the east where the decisive battles of the war were to be fought.

The war in the east — and in the west

Hitler now turned his attention to the east. Ostensibly he was still on friendly terms with the Russian dictator, Stalin, and the two were co-operating in the exploitation of eastern Europe. But Hitler was now making plans to realize the dream of *Mein Kampf* — a European empire stretching as far as the Ural Mountains and all working for the benefit of the Aryan supermen. However, he was to delay the attack on Russia in order to subdue other areas of eastern Europe which were giving him trouble. In March 1941 the Italian dictator, Mussolini, needed Hitler's help to subdue Greece, on which he had launched an attack in October 1940. The political upheavals in Yugoslavia in early 1941 with the fall of the pro-German government in that country meant that Hitler needed to extend the attack there too. And, again, in the North African War the Italians needed reinforcements. Mussolini had hoped that this would be an easy war with lots of pickings, but he was finding that he had taken on more than he could handle. Many experts think that being forced by these concerns to delay his attack on Russia was one major reason why Hitler lost the war.

Hitler and Mussolini often met during those years on the Brenner Pass between Austria and Italy, or in Salzburg. Hitler, the German dictator, more than ever master of the situation, delivered endless lectures to Mussolini, the Italian dictator, who was ever more humiliated. Italian Foreign Minister, Ciano, noted in his diary:

> Hitler talks, talks, talks. Mussolini suffers — he, who is in the habit of talking himself, and who, instead, practically has to keep quiet. On the second day, after lunch, when everything had been said, Hitler talked uninterruptedly for an hour and forty minutes. He omitted absolutely no

argument: war and peace, religion and philosophy, art and history. Mussolini automatically looked at his wrist watch . . .

But by the summer of 1941 these days of waiting were at last over. The Soviet dictator, Stalin, had been warned from many sources of Hitler's intentions of attack, and massive German forces were building up in occupied Poland, but astonishingly he took no notice. Hitler was confident of victory. He said: "The world will hold its breath and make no comment".

The attack was launched on 22 June 1941: with incredible swiftness German troops moved across the vast Russian plains and it seemed for a while as if another lightning war was in progress. "Operation Barbarossa" was the fulfilment of Hitler's chief dream and he expressed his relief that the final decision to attack Russia had now been made in a letter to Mussolini:

> Since I struggled through to this decision, I again feel spiritually free. The partnership with the Soviet Union, in spite of the complete sincerity of my efforts to bring about a final conciliation, was nevertheless often very irksome to me, for in some way or other it seemed to me to be a break with my whole origin, my concepts and my former obligations. I am happy now to be delivered from this torment.

It was the most fateful decision of his life.

As winter approached, the easy victory he had hoped for did not come. His refusal to concentrate his attack, the vast spaces of Russia, and the determined defence of their homeland by the Soviet people (spurred on by the increasingly brutal methods and use of mass murder by the German armies and the SS) were all factors in this. Towards Christmas the German armies had almost reached Moscow, but now the harsh Russian winter

41 The Blitzkrieg hits Russia, but here it is to encounter its first failure.

hampered their efforts. The Russians launched their first important counter-attack in December 1941 under Marshal Zhukov; it was the beginning of a long bloody war which was to result in the Germans' being finally cleared from Soviet soil three years later.

In that same December month, Hitler made another fateful and disastrous decision. For some time Japan had been growing closer to the "Axis" side of Italy and Germany and the United States of America closer to the "Allies", Britain, France and (since the attack on her) the Soviet Union. But America and Japan were not in open conflict. Then on 7 December 1941 the Japanese attacked the Americans at Pearl Harbour. Hitler had previously had great patience with the American government which was giving considerable help to Britain. But a few days after the Pearl Harbour attack Hitler declared war on the United States, in alliance with Japan. Hitler knew little of America except that it was a great racial mixture; this factor led him to underestimate its strength. Moreover, it seems that as the years went on his plans were growing ever wider; it was no longer only a great European empire he wanted, but a world one. In July 1941 he had spoken to the Japanese ambassador, who reported on the conversation:

The United States and England will always be our enemies. This realization must be

42 German infantry in Russia.

43 This American cartoon about Hitler's imperialistic methods appeared as early as 1933. It seems an accurate prophecy.

the basis of our foreign policy . . . . Therefore he [Hitler] was of the opinion that we must jointly destroy them.

Hitler's declaring war on the United States was the great turning-point of the war. Hitler had now taken on a combination of forces which must ultimately destroy him; his arrogance had finally got the better of him. From then on his conduct of the war shows an increasing failure to manage its overall strategy on such a variety of fronts. 1942 was the year fortune began to turn against Hitler. The Americans gained the upper hand in the Far Eastern War, Hitler began to lose the U-boat war in the Pacific, the North African war was turned in favour of the Allies at El Alamein in October 1942 and, closest of all to Hitler's heart, the attempt to capture Stalingrad in the winter of 1942-3 failed with the loss of a whole German army. Hitler raged and fulminated, but he had nobody but himself whom he could justly blame.

Hitler and the "New Order" in Europe

Nevertheless, by the end of 1941 Hitler had become master of almost the whole of Europe. He had come a long way indeed from the penniless tramp of the Vienna days, when he had first learnt to hate. In the countries he had conquered various methods of Nazi control were imposed. Some areas, often those inhabited by the hated Slavs, were ruled directly by the Nazis and were reserved for the most brutal exploitation. Some governments were in alliance with the Nazis and had to contribute to the German war effort. Others were officially neutral but could not defy Germany. In the grandiose Chancellory that he had had built for himself Hitler received the subject-rulers of eastern Europe, Prince Paul of Yugoslavia, Marshal Antonescu of Romania and others, and confronted them with demands for more money or more labourers to work in the German factories. Defiance would have been unwise;

44   A typical prisoner of war camp.

when King Boris of Bulgaria died suddenly after a visit to Hitler's headquarters in 1943, there were dark rumours of murder. Of all European dictators only Franco, the Spanish dictator, seemed able to resist Hitler, refusing all invitations to take part in Hitler's war.

But it was in Russia that Hitler's plans for the "new order" were most clearly seen and that the most determined attempt was made to put the Nazi *Weltanschauung* into practice. Hitler had made it plain that he wanted full-scale racial war to the death in Russia, in order to secure for the Germans the *Lebensraum* he considered they needed. He had told the army leaders in March 1941:

> The war against Russia will be such that it cannot be conducted in a knightly fashion. This struggle is one of ideological and racial differences and will have to be conducted with unprecedented, unmerciful and unrelenting harshness . . .

It was the SS, headed by their bespectacled chieftain Heinrich Himmler, who were mainly concerned with executing the racial policies in the east. Special detachments, the *Einsatzgruppen*, went into Russia behind the army with orders to exterminate Communist Party officials, resisters and Jews; one group was responsible for the deaths of more than 90,000 in a few weeks. Russian prisoners of war were treated with utmost brutality; three million of them are thought to have died in captivity. Many a German mother, too, lost her son in this war of blood and snow. Perhaps more than twenty million people died on the Russian front: the exact number can never be known. Within Germany millions of slave labourers toiled so that this war effort could be kept in operation.

What was it all for? Hitler had a dream of a new German empire in the east — a "thousand year Reich" — where heroic German settlers would live on huge farms along straight roads, protected by military

installations, and served as slaves by the inferior races of the east. At his headquarters or at his home in the Bavarian mountains Hitler would talk endlessly to his associates about his plans:

This Russian desert, we shall populate it . . . . We'll take away its character of an Asiatic steppe, we'll Europeanize it. With this object we have undertaken the construction of roads that will lead to the southernmost part of the Crimea and to the Caucasus. These roads will be studded along their whole length with

German towns and around these towns our colonists will settle . . .

At their most pretentious the Nazis claimed that they would be creating a "new man" on the steppes, giving the Aryan superman his fullest chance to develop. It did not matter to Hitler that the average German had no wish to emigrate to icy Russia or that he had very little idea what the German would actually do when he was established on his farm surrounded by his Slavic slaves. The Nazis got very little time, in fact, to carry out their colonization plans, but they certainly

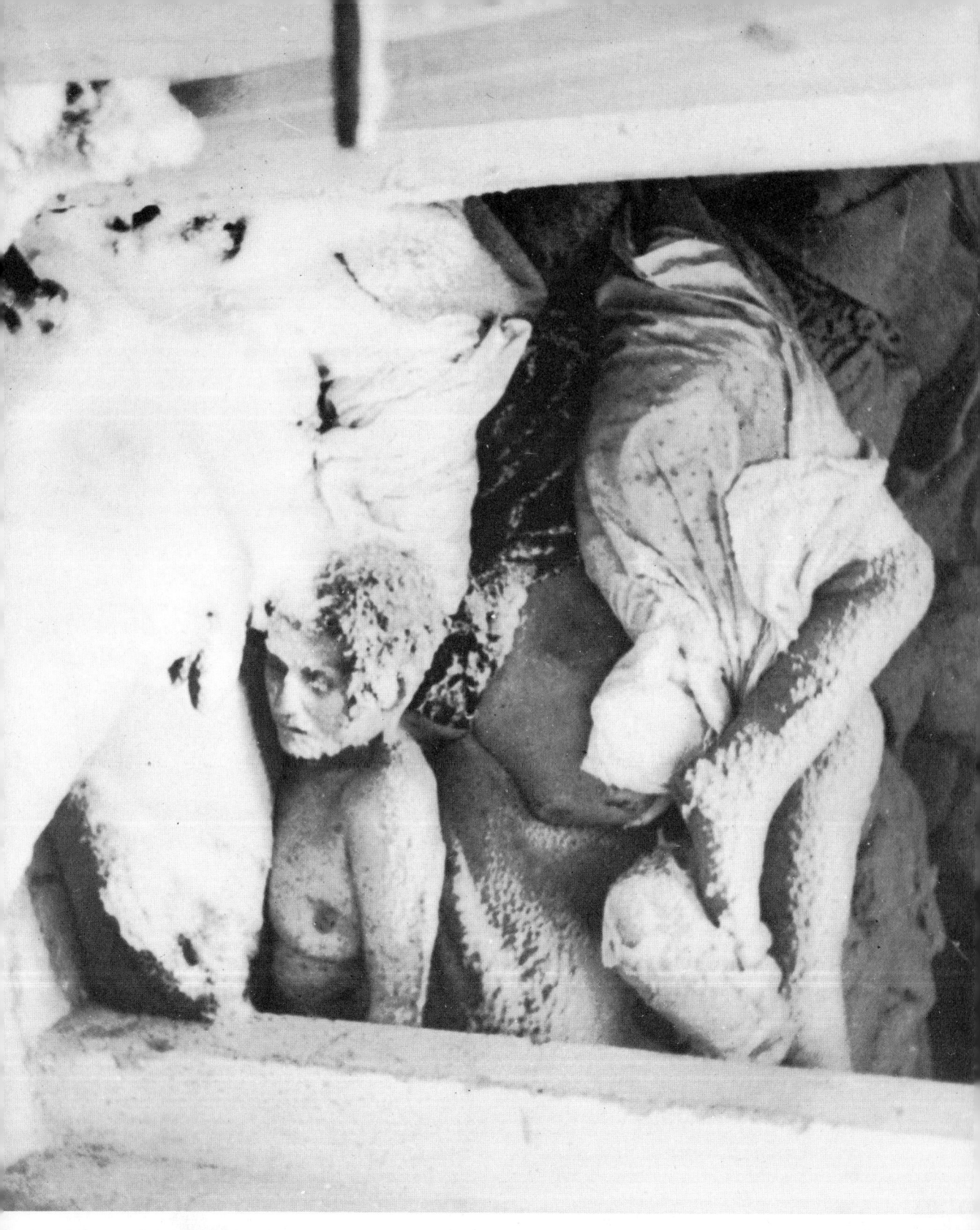

45   The inside of a gas chamber.

got the chance to murder millions to make their perverted dream come true.

Hitler and the extermination of the Jews

Hitler's greatest hatred, the greatest of many, had always been of the Jews. In his teeming imagination the Jew was the devil figure capable of any wickedness, not really human and not fit to live. Anti-semitism (anti-Jewishness) had long been a tradition in both Germany and Europe generally; it had been especially bad in eastern Europe and in Vienna where Hitler had picked it up as a young man. But for hundreds of years in Germany there had been no mass murders of Jews, and the Nazi decision, gradually arrived at, to exterminate the Jewish race in Europe, was therefore a reversion to levels of barbarity which Europe thought it had left behind in the Middle Ages. Mass murders of Jews began during the early years of the war when the Nazis had a large number of the Jews of Europe at their mercy. First, the Jews were taken in large numbers to country districts and shot down. Later they were gassed in mobile vans; and from 1942 there were several extermination camps, all situated in Poland, equipped with gas chambers and crematoria to burn the bodies. About six million Jews and others (principally gypsies) were exterminated in total. Here an eyewitness describes a mass shooting of Jews:

> I walked round a mound of earth and stood before the gigantic grave. People lay so closely pressed together that only their heads could be seen. Blood was running from almost all the heads across the shoulders. Many of those who had been shot were still moving. Some raised their arms and turned their heads to show that they were still alive. The pit was already two-thirds full. I estimated that it contained about a thousand people. I looked round for the marksman. It was an SS man sitting on the edge of the short side of the pit, his legs hanging down into it; on his knees lay a submachine gun, and he was smoking a cigarette. The people, entirely naked, walked down some steps which had been dug into the clay wall of the pit, and then slid across the heads of those who lay there until they reached the place which the SS-man had pointed out to them. They lay down in front of the dead or wounded, some were stroking those still alive and talking to them quietly. Then I heard a series of shots. I looked into the pit and saw bodies moving convulsively or heads which were lying quite still on the bodies in front. Blood poured from the napes of the necks.

These terrible piles of bodies were to be Hitler's chief monument. The extermination plans emerged in gradual stages and were master-minded chiefly by the SS leaders, Himmler and Heydrich, and the local SS chiefs in the occupied eastern territories. The whole business was kept top secret; the camps were all in Poland and every effort was made to keep knowledge of them from the German population. On this basis, an English historian, David Irving, has recently attempted to argue that Hitler himself did not know about the extermination of the Jews, but there is no good evidence for such an argument and it is unconvincing. For a start it is inherently improbable; Hitler was supreme in Germany and this was one of the most important actions of the state. Hitler was fiercely anti-semitic, even by Nazi standards. He publicly boasted on several occasions that he would exterminate the Jews. Dr Goebbels in his diary for 1942 makes it quite clear that Hitler was fully aware of the fate of the Jews:

> The Führer once more expressed his determination to clean up the Jews in Europe pitilessly. There must be no more squeamish sentimentalism about it . . . . Their destruction will go hand in hand with the destruction of our enemies.

46 Hitler with the Chiefs of Staff of the Armed Forces pores over maps of the front.

Even to the very end of the war the gas-chambers went on relentlessly killing on the orders of the mad Führer. It was his most savage act of destruction. His crimes against humanity were many, but it is this deed above all that will make him rank as one of the greatest criminals of all time.

Hitler's life during the war

During the war Hitler's routine changed. Previously he had wasted much time endlessly talking or eating cakes in Munich coffee-shops. He had had rages, but in good moods he had been approachable. During the war he became a terrifying despot, distant and concerned only with winning the war. He spent little time in Germany and made few speeches to the people; much of his time was spent in his headquarters on the Russian Front or at his east-Prussian headquarters, a bare, uncomfortable place set among dark woods, which was known as "The Wolf's Lair". Endlessly he pored over maps and official papers. He had few pleasures now; for a time he listened to music, but as the war-news grew ever worse, he stopped doing even that. Goebbels said:

It is tragic that the Führer has become such a recluse and leads such an unhealthy life. He never gets out into the fresh air. He does not relax. He sits in his bunker, worries and broods. If only one could transfer him to other surroundings! . . .

Goebbels thought that Hitler's Alsatian dog, Blondi, was closer to him than any human being.

The life Hitler lived was unhealthy in other ways too. He placed great faith in a quack doctor called Morell who prescribed for him an incredible collection of drugs. Neither his mental nor his physical health had ever been good, and under the pressure of directing a world war it grew worse and worse. The attempt on his life by a bomb in 1944 wounded him and this further weakened his constitution. By 1945 Hitler was an entirely broken man who could not walk more than twenty yards at any one time. Speer writes of his last days:

> Now he was stumbling like an old man. His limbs trembled; he walked stooped, with dragging footsteps . . . his uniform, which in the past he had kept scrupulously neat, was often neglected in this last period of his life and stained by the food he had eaten with a shaking hand.

And this was a man in his mid-fifties! One thing only remained constant in the wreck of Hitler: his immense egomaniac will. He was determined to fight on and, if he fell, to bring Germany down with him.

Hitler's war and the Germans

The Germans had never, except in the days of great victories, been enthusiastic about the war. In the early days, with the rest of Europe being plundered, few sacrifices had been demanded of them, but after Speer became Minister of Armaments in 1942 they were forced to work much harder to keep the war going. They rarely heard or saw Hitler, but they knew that the atmosphere of terror had grown so great that a mere careless word could bring them death. From the middle of the war onwards British and American bombers came nightly over their cities and ever more horrific destruction was caused; by the end of the war many cities had been practically bombed out of existence. It was becoming increasingly obvious by the year 1943 that the war was lost.

But there was no revolt in Germany and little complaining. Why was this? Perhaps the atmosphere of terror had become too great. The Germans had a long-standing tradition of obedience to authority which made revolt difficult for them. Also the experience of Hitler had been hypnotic and there was a widespread feeling that, disastrous as he had been for them, he represented the country's fate. So they waited patiently and hopelessly until the whole business came to a stop. It is perhaps surprising, even so, that they could not make a successful effort to rid themselves of the tyrant. Late in the war a German writer wrote in his diary:

> You, my readers, who will have these lines before you only at some later time, can you grasp it, that such a thing was possible? That our German people in all calmness . . . looked on, while a pack of fools, against whom destiny had long since decided, let the whole wonderful Reich be transformed into one single garbage heap? In the end, even jewels like Freiburg, Würzburg, Heilbronn, Dresden, and all the others!

There was only one major attempt to get rid of Hitler — in 1944 — and that sprang mainly from the officers of the German army who alone possessed the force to stage a successful take-over from the Nazis. (There were also a few courageous individual protesters against Hitler, like Hans and Sophie Scholl, who were executed for distributing leaflets against the evil regime.) Only a minority of army officers were in the plot and besides them a looser-knit group of clergy, diplomats, secret servicemen and aristocrats. The plot was quite wide-ranging but had few connections with the mass of Germans. The conspirators, who represented conservative forces in Germany, hoped to negotiate a compromise peace with the Allies whereby Germany would be allowed to keep at least a few of her gains; failing that, they planned to unconditionally surrender as the Allies wanted. On 20 July 1944 a courageous and brilliant young officer, Claus von Stauffenberg, who had access to Hitler's east Prussian headquarters, planted a bomb there during a meeting. By great luck Hitler escaped with his life, although he was wounded and several people at the meeting were killed. The attempt at take-over of Germany was quelled by quick Nazi thinking, the hesitation of the conspirators and by the voice of Hitler, still alive, speaking over the radio:

If I speak to you today it is first in order that you should hear my voice and should know that I am unhurt and well, and, secondly, that you should hear of a crime unparalleled in German history. A very small clique of ambitious, irresponsible and, at the same time, senseless and stupid officers, had concocted a plot to eliminate me . . .

The scale of Hitler's vengeance after the attempt proved that it had indeed been more than a "very small clique" who had tried to kill Hitler. Stauffenberg had been shot the day of the conspiracy; hundreds more were executed, often in a horrible manner; and thousands more, who were merely under suspicion of being connected with the plot or had family members connected with it, were sent to concentration camps.

47 Hitler visits the sick after the attempt on his life in July 1944, which killed four men and wounded several others.

The war on the turn

Hitler was determined never to surrender whatever the losses. At the end of January 1943 the German Sixth Army at the Battle of Stalingrad, frozen, starving and with almost all its men lost, had surrendered under Paulus to the Russians. They could hardly have fought on, but Hitler was furious, launching great tirades against Paulus:

> The man should have shot himself just as the old commanders who threw themselves on their swords when they saw that the cause was lost.

Later in 1943 the Italian dictator, Mussolini, was deposed; the Germans later set him up as a puppet ruler in a part of Italy of which they still had control. In 1944 German armies were cleared from Russian soil and in 1945 the Russians were entering Poland, finding the horrific remains of the extermination camps. In June 1944 the Anglo-American armies landed in France and in August they liberated Paris. Their demand of the Germans was unconditional surrender and any reasonable ruler would have given in. But Hitler was determined that, if the German people had proved unworthy of his plans for them, everything should be destroyed. As the Allied armies entered German soil, Hitler gave orders for a "scorched earth" policy — that even more of Germany should be destroyed to hamper the enemy who was bound to win. In March 1945 he said:

> If the war is to be lost, the nation will also perish. This fate is inevitable. There is no need to consider the basis of even a most primitive existence any longer. On the contrary, it is better to destroy even that, and to destroy it ourselves. The nation has proved itself weak, and the future belongs solely to the stronger eastern nations. Besides, those who remain after the battle are of little value; for the good have fallen.

These orders, in fact, were followed only in part; the spell was beginning to break. But Hitler was to be in control to the bitter end.

Hitler's ruin

In early 1945, with Berlin in total ruins around him and the Russians at the outskirts of the city, Hitler and a few close associates retired to an underground bunker beneath the ruined Chancellery. Here he flew into violent rages, gave orders to attack to units that no longer existed, and sometimes broke into fits of weeping. To the end he was hoping for a miraculous rescue and was furious when some of the other leaders, Göring and Himmler, tried to reach last-minute agreements with the Allies. By the last week of April the Russians were within the city and the end was within sight. The news arrived that the Italian dictator Mussolini had been caught by resistance fighters, shot, and hung up by his heels in a petrol station. Hitler was determined to avoid a similar fate.

Eva Braun had flown in to share the Führer's fate whatever it might be. One day before he killed himself she had her reward for all the years of neglect: Hitler made her his wife. It was one of his few generous acts, but the Political Testament that he dictated before his death shows that his mind was still as full of hatred and resentment as it had always been. He never thought to blame himself for the catastrophe; it was everyone else who had failed him. But most of all he blamed those whom he had always regarded as his greatest enemies — the Jews. In his mind they remained the eternal scapegoats:

> It is untrue that I or anyone else in Germany wanted war in 1939. It was wanted and provoked solely by international statesmen either of Jewish origin or working for Jewish interests.

On the afternoon of 30 April 1945 Hitler and Eva Braun, having said goodbye to the men and women in the bunker, went into a private room and killed themselves. Eva took poison;

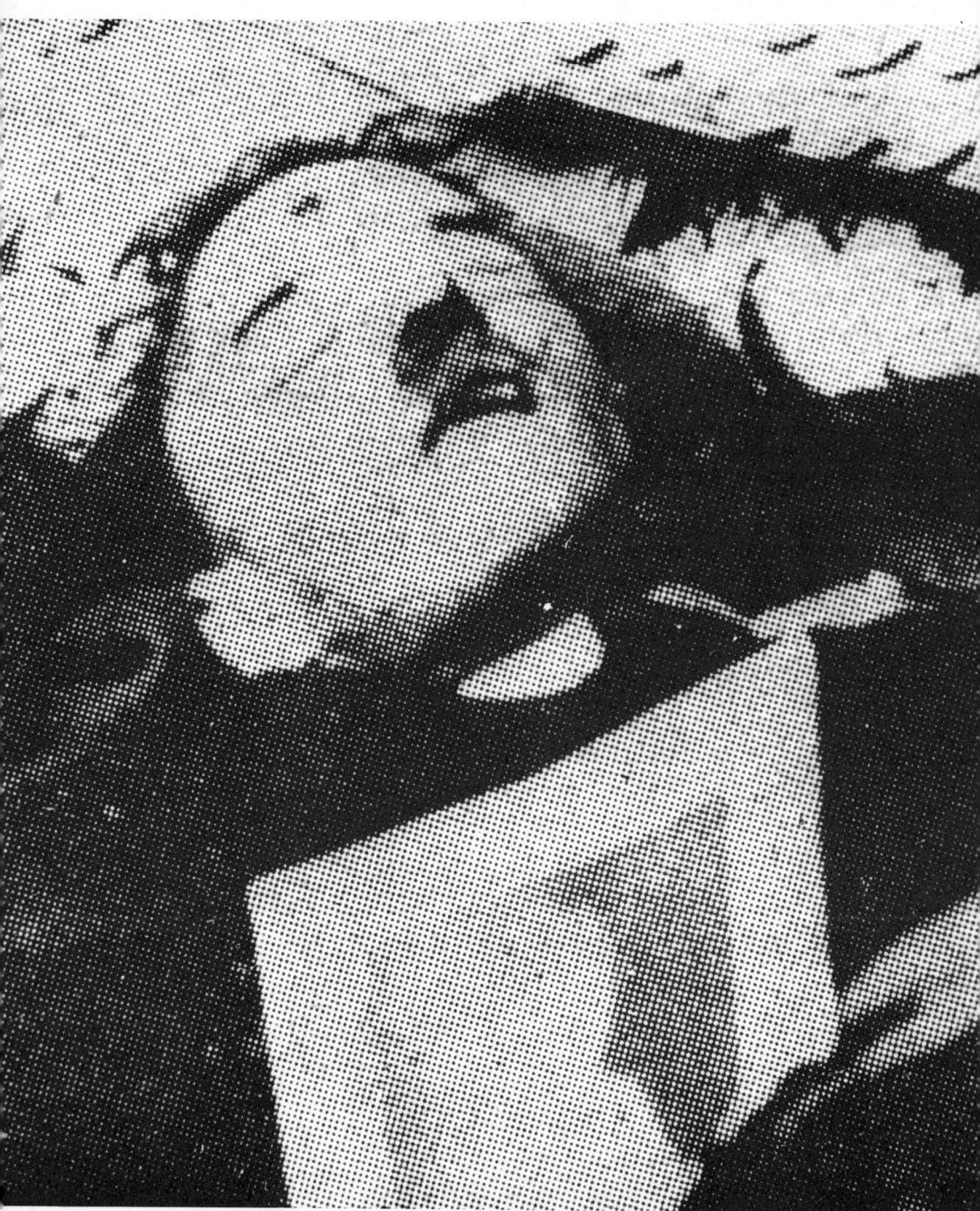

it is uncertain whether Hitler shot himself or whether he took posion and then Eva shot him to make it appear a hero's death. Their bodies were burnt according to Nazi ceremony, but the Russians later discovered Hitler's remains. Just one week later the Third Reich surrendered unconditionally to the Allies.

The aftermath

The Third Reich disappeared without trace and little of Hitler's work can be seen in Germany today. His ideology is utterly discredited and the dream of German greatness and rule over the continent is gone for ever; the two great powers now are the Soviet Union and the United States, one communist and one capitalist, which stepped into the power-vacuum left by the defeat of Germany. Hitler's work had an impact, but it was purely destructive. It was only after his regime had been destroyed that more positive political movements could be built. The vast population movements after 1945, when millions of Germans were expelled from eastern Europe, and the fact that Germany is now a permanently divided country are both examples of destructive results of Hitler's rule. But his most enduring monument is the terrible toll of suffering and the millions dead. He had been the product of an evil period in history and, once it had passed, his movement and his ideas had absolutely nothing to offer. Traudl Junge, Hitler's secretary, wrote two decades later:

> Hitler's death released us from a state of mass hypnosis. Suddenly we rediscovered that we possessed an irresistible urge to live, to be ourselves, to be human beings. Hitler was no longer of any interest to us.

48 This picture is said to have been taken by a member of Hitler's staff shortly before the body was ceremoniously burnt. The remains later examined by the Russians are now generally accepted to be those of Hitler after his corpse was burnt.

List of Dates of Hitler's Activities

Hitler's Formative Years (pages 9-20)

1889	20 April	Hitler born at Braunau am Inn, Austria.
1903	January	Death of Alois Hitler, Hitler's father.
1905	September	Hitler leaves school at sixteen without a leaving certificate.
1907	October	Hitler takes the entrance exam for the Vienna Academy of Fine Arts without success.
1908	December	Death of Klara Hitler, Hitler's mother, leaving Hitler a small legacy and an orphan's pension.
1909	November	Hitler forced by lack of money to abandon his furnished room and take to the streets.
1913	May	Hitler moves to Munich in Germany.
1914	August	On the outbreak of the First World War, fought between Germany and Austria on the one side and France, Britain and Russia on the other, Hitler petitions the Bavarian King to serve in a Bavarian regiment, a request which is granted.
1916	October	Hitler is wounded by a grenade splinter and hospitalized in Germany.
1918	August	Hitler is awarded the Iron Cross (First Class), a high military decoration.
	October	Hitler is wounded by British gas poisoning, temporarily losing his sight.
	November	First World War ends with the defeat of Germany and Austria; the two empires collapse. In the shock of this moment, Hitler decides to go into politics.

Leader in Waiting (pages 21-35)

1919	January	German Workers' Party is founded in Munich by Anton Drexler, one of many new political groupings at this time.
	June	Versailles Peace Treaty signed with harsh conditions for Germany.
	September	Hitler attends his first meeting of the German Workers' Party.
1920	February	First mass-meeting of the party at the Munich Hofbräuhaus,

now called the National Socialist German Workers' Party (Nazis).

1921	July	Hitler becomes Chairman of the Party and Führer.
1923	January	Occupation of the Ruhr by the French signals a period of crisis in Germany.
	8 November	Hitler leads the unsuccessful "Beer-Hall Putsch".
1924	February	Hitler's trial for treason begins, and he is later sent to Landsberg Prison.
	April	Hitler begins to dictate *Mein Kampf*.
	December	Hitler is released from prison.
1925	July	Publication of the first volume of *Mein Kampf*.
	October	Signature of Locarno Pact between Germany and the western powers signals period of calm in Germany.
1928	May	At Reichstag elections, Nazis receive 2.5 per cent of the vote, 12 out of 491 seats.
1929	October	The Wall Street Crash; a period of economic depression begins.
1930	September	Nazis get 18 per cent of the vote, 107 out of 571 seats.
1931	September	Nazi vote doubled in the state of Hesse.
1932	February	Hitler takes out German citizenship.
	July	Nazis with 37 per cent of the vote, 230 out of 608 seats.
	August	Hitler refuses a Cabinet post.
	November	Nazis with 32 per cent of the vote, 196 out of 608 seats.
1933	January	Hitler is appointed Chancellor by Hindenburg as the result of intrigue.
	28 February	The Reichstag fire; state of emergency imposed. Reichstag elections give the Nazis 288 out of 647 seats, 44 per cent of the vote.
	March	Reichstag votes by large majority to terminate its own powers.

Hitler, the Peacetime Leader (pages 36-51)

1933	March-July	Process of *Gleichshaltung* in progress.
	October	Germany withdraws from the League of Nations.
1934	January	Ten-year non-aggression pact signed between Germany and Poland.
	June	The Blood-Purge or "The Night of the Long Knives"; Röhm and other SA leaders shot.
	August	Death of Hindenburg; Hitler becomes President himself as well as Chancellor.
1935	March	Conscription introduced in Germany.
	June	Anglo-German Naval Agreement.
	September	Nürnberg Laws take away German citizenship from Jews.
1936	March	Hitler marches into Rhineland.
	October	Rome-Berlin Axis formed by Hitler and Mussolini.
1937	November	Hitler calls the Hossbach Conference of his chief advisers to outline his plans for empire.
1938	March	Hitler and the Nazis take over Austria.
	April	Sudeten Germans call for autonomy from Czechoslovakia.

	September	The Munich Conference results in cession of the Sudetenland to Germany.
	November	"Crystal Night": pogrom against the Jews with much damage to property and loss of several hundred Jewish lives.
1939	March	Hitler takes over Czechoslovakia.
		British and French governments guarantee the security of Poland.
	May	Hitler informs his generals that war is "inevitable".
	August	Nazi-Soviet Pact signed.
	3 September	Second World War begins with Britain, France and Poland on the one side and Germany and the Soviet Union on the other.

Hitler as Warlord (pages 60-79)

1939	September	Poland is overrun.
		Jews in Germany are forbidden to be out after 8 o'clock in summer, 9 o'clock in winter; just one measure in a mounting campaign of persecution.
1940	May	Main offensive in the west begins.
	June	Fall of France to Nazis under Hitler.
	July-September	Battle of Britain.
1941	March	Nazi attack on Yugoslavia and Greece.
	June	Hitler invades the Soviet Union; Soviet Union joins the Allies.
	September	General deportation of the Jews eastwards from Germany begins.
	December	First Russian counter-offensive near Moscow.
		Hitler declares war on the United States in alliance with Japan.
1942	June	First mass gassings of Jews at Auschwitz extermination camp.
1943	January	Surrender of German Sixth Army at Stalingrad marks chief turning-point of the war.
	July	Fall of Mussolini as Italian dictator.
1944	July	The bomb-plot against Hitler fails.
	September	Invasion of Germany from the west.
	October	Belgrade falls to the Russians.
1945	February	British and American armies cross the Rhine.
	April	Russians enter Berlin.
		Hitler and Eva Braun commit suicide.
	May	Third Reich surrenders unconditionally to the Allies.

Biographical Notes on Hitler's Contemporaries

Braun, Eva. Born 1912 in Munich, the daughter of a schoolteacher. She was employed in her late teens as a model by Hoffmann, Hitler's court photographer, and he brought her to Hitler's attention. She was Hitler's mistress during the whole period of the Third Reich but rarely appeared in public. A simple girl who liked sports and entertainments, Eva Braun had no political importance but added a certain amount of relaxation to Hitler's life. She was married to Hitler on 29 June 1945 and committed suicide with him the next day.

Drexler, Anton. Born in Munich in 1884, Drexler was the founder of the German Workers' Party, the small political grouping from which the Nazi Party sprang. He was a locksmith, a humble man with confused political ideas. He soon lost influence in the party to Hitler and left it in 1923. There was a reconciliation in 1930, but Drexler died in 1942, having taken no real part in the Nazi movement for twenty years.

Goebbels, Josef. Born in 1897 in Rheydt in the Rhineland, the son of a manual worker. He studied at various universities and joined the Nazi Party in 1922. During the 1920s he worked rather unsuccessfully in journalism, but in 1926 he was made Nazi *Gauleiter* (local leader) in Berlin where he proved to have great organizational talents and founded the Nazi newspaper *Der Angriff* (The Attack). He was Nazi Propaganda Chief from 1929 and was appointed Minister of Propaganda in 1933. He was responsible for developing very effective propaganda control over people's lives and during the war he was largely responsible for building up morale on the home front. He committed suicide, the day after Hitler, with his wife in the bunker; at the same time the couple poisoned their six children.

Göring, Hermann. Born 1893 at Rosenheim, the son of a high colonial official who became the first Governor of German South-West Africa. Göring was a famous air-ace in the First World War, winning many medals. After the war he found it difficult to settle down, but joined the Party in 1922 and was wounded in the attempted Putsch of 1923. He was the chief Nazi political agent in Berlin in the early 1930s establishing contact with influential social circles. Once the Nazis were in power, he received a host of important appointments: Prussian Minister President, Plenipotentiary for the Four Year Plan, Reich Minister for Air, Prussian Minister of Interior and so on. He lost influence during the war years. Ruthless and popular, Göring was handicapped by laziness, too great a love of luxury and drug addiction. He was con-

49 Hitler with Josef Goebbels (centre) and Hermann Göring (right).

demned to be hanged at the Nuremberg Trials in 1946, but committed suicide in his cell before the execution could take place.

Hess, Rudolf. Born 1884 in Alexandria in Egypt, the son of a German importer there. Hess fought in the First World War and joined the Party in its early days. He became Private Secretary to Hitler in 1925. A solemn, rather stupid man, Hess was made Deputy Leader in 1933. In May 1941, although loyal to Hitler, he took off in a private 'plane for Scotland on a peace mission to the British, but was imprisoned by them. He was condemned at the Nuremberg Tribunal in 1946 to life imprisonment for war crimes and has been in Spandau prison, near Berlin, ever since.

Heydrich, Reinhard. Born 1904 in Halle, the son of the founder of the Halle Conservatory of Music. He was a naval officer in the 1920s, but was cashiered in 1931 for having an affair with the wife of a higher officer. IN 1932 he joined the SS and rose swiftly within that organization; in 1936 he was the Chief of the Security Police and Security Service (SD) and second to Himmler within the SS. Called by Hitler "The Man with the Iron Heart", Heydrich was a tall, blond, totally ruthless planner of terror and one of the chief organizers of the extermination of the Jews. He was assassinated in Prague in 1942 by Czech resistance fighters: a whole Czech village was massacred by the Nazis in revenge.

Himmler, Heinrich. Born 1900 in Munich, the son of a secondary school teacher. He took part in the attempted Putsch of 1923. In 1928 he became a poultry farmer at which he was unsuccessful, but in 1929 he became the head of the SS, originally Hitler's bodyguard, but which he wielded into a highly effective terror and fighting machine. By 1936 he was the head of all police services in

84

Germany and during the war he was the chief executor, as head of the SS, of the racial policies in the east. Bespectacled and insignificant-looking, Himmler was one of the greatest mass murderers of all time. He committed suicide in British captivity in 1945 by swallowing poison.

Hindenburg, Paul von. Born at Posen in 1847 into an aristocratic Prussian family, Hindenburg had a long and successful army career and retired in 1911. At the outbreak of war in 1914 he was recalled and became Chief Commander in the east and General Field Marshal. He became President of the Weimar Republic in 1925 and in this position, old and confused, offered Hitler the Chancellorship in 1933. He died in 1934 and his office was taken over by Hitler.

Rauschning, Hermann. Born in Thorn in 1887, Rauschning came from an old Prussian noble family. He was a lieutenant in the First World War and joined the Nazi Party in 1932, shortly afterwards becoming a member of the Danzig Senate (equivalent to a British town council) and a trusted confidant of Hitler, who seems to have poured out his most secret beliefs to him. As a result, Rauschning became an anti-Nazi and fled to Switzerland in 1936, later writing several books in which he tried to put forward the true character of Nazi aims. From 1948 Rauschning became a farmer in Oregon, USA.

Röhm, Ernst. Born 1887 in Munich, the son of a civil servant. Röhm was a professional soldier and Hitler's most useful link in early days with army circles; he was one of the earliest members of the Party. He organized the SA, the Nazi private army, but in the 1920s, rather discontented, he emigrated to Bolivia. He was recalled by Hitler in 1930 to take charge of the SA, but in 1934 he and other SA leaders were executed by Hitler in

"The Night of the Long Knives" because it was thought that they might stage a plot against the leadership of the Party.

Schleicher, Kurt von. Born in 1882, and from a Prussian noble family, Schleicher followed the traditional career for his class of going into the army. In the 1920s he became known as a political general who wielded great influence behind the scenes of German politics but rarely came into the limelight. He was one of the chief conservative figures who toyed with the idea of giving Hitler a share in power in order to tame him, and he was the last Chancellor of the German Republic before Hitler took power, being Chancellor for two months in December 1932 and January 1933. He soon paid the penalty of his political misjudgement; suspected of plotting against Hitler, he was executed in June 1934 at the same time as the purge of the SA called "The Night of the Long Knives".

Speer, Albert. Born in Mannheim in 1905, son of an architect. He followed his father's profession and studied at the Berlin Technical College; he joined the Party in 1931 after

51   Hitler talks to Speer (left).

hearing Hitler make a speech. He became Hitler's favourite architect and designed many buildings for him; in 1942 he was appointed Minister of Armaments and proved himself a great organizing success. He was condemned at the Nuremberg Tribunal to twenty years' imprisonment and was released in 1966. Since then, through various books, he has been successful in spreading his own, probably not always accurate, version of events in the Third Reich.

Spengler, Oswald. Born in 1880, Spengler first studied at various universities, then became a schoolteacher, then devoted himself to writing, producing his major work *The Decline of the West (Der Untergang des Abendlandes)* between 1918 and 1922. Spengler was typical of the generation of German intellectuals who rejected democracy and preached strong-arm methods, who are said to have helped create a climate for Nazism to flourish. But he later reacted against the crudities and inhuman urge for power in the Nazi government and, as a private citizen, became openly critical of the Nazi regime. Probably only his death in 1936 saved him from persecution by the Nazis.

Stauffenberg, Claus von. Stauffenberg was born in 1907 into a family of the south German nobility and followed a career in the Army General Staff. Brilliant, handsome, daring and inspired by Christian principles, Stauffenberg, after being seriously wounded in 1943 and loosing a hand, still became a leading member of the widespread conspiracy against Hitler and himself planted the bomb on 20 July 1944 at Hitler's headquarters which coincided with the military revolt against Hitler. Hitler was unhurt and the revolt failed. Stauffenberg, with three others, was executed by firing squad in Berlin that same night.

52   Claus von Stauffenberg, a leading member of the conspiracy against Hitler.

Glossary

Anti-semitism
Prejudice against Jews. The Jews are, strictly, not a race but a cultural and religious community; they are not all members of the semitic population group who are grouped in the Middle Eastern area. Thus to be pre-

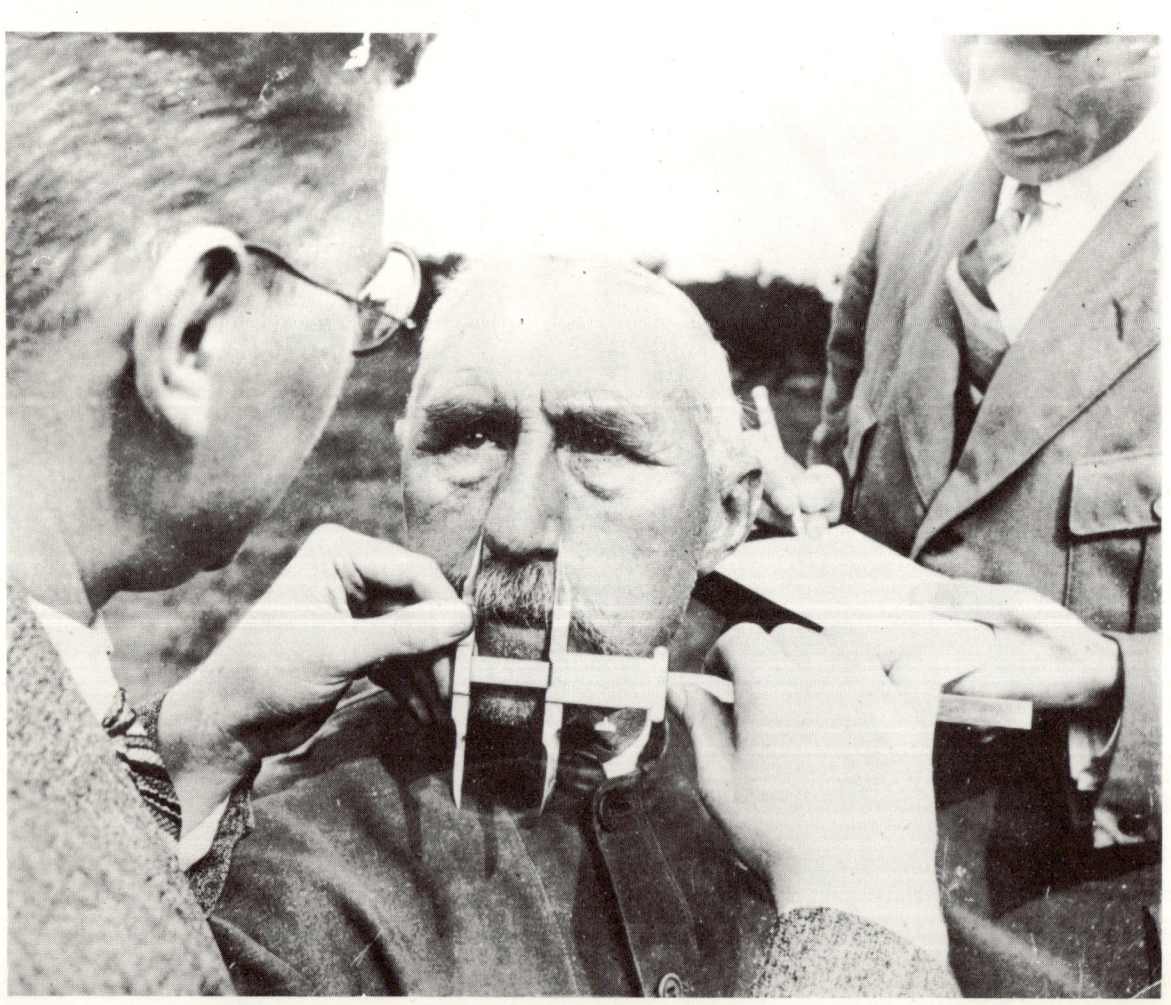

judiced against the Jews as a "race", as the Nazis were, was based on a lack of understanding. The Jews had formed separate communities in Europe for thousands of years before the Nazis; they had often aroused prejudice because they could be distinguished from their neighbours and often followed different occupations. Hitler's mass extermination of the Jews was the horrifying climax of centuries of persecution, but took place after a period when the position of Jews in Europe had seemed to be improving.

Appeasement
The policy adopted by several western statesmen who believed that the dictators, Hitler and Mussolini, had some just grievances and could be rendered harmless if their demands were met. Appeasement was based on a widespread feeling that some nations, especially Germany, had been treated unfairly after the First World War. It was an honourable, sincere policy, but it failed to understand that dictators like Hitler and Mussolini could not be appeased in this way.

Aryan
It used to be believed that the world could be divided up into three great racial groups: Caucasian (Aryan), Mongoloid and Negroid; this idea has now been abandoned by most scholars who think in terms of mixed population groups. The Nazis did not even use the word in this semi-scientific way; they used the word to mean a supposed north European master race, principally composed of Germans. Roughly, this idea corresponds to the idea of the Nordic population group. But the Germans are, in fact, the most mixed population of Europe in their origin and any idea that people are superior because of their race is false.

53 The width of this man's nose is measured to determine his race.

Concentration camps
These were the prison camps that the Nazi regime set up for all those it believed to be enemies of the state; these included communists, socialists, pacifists, criminals, homosexuals and the mentally ill. Torture and murder were common in these camps, but they were not specifically set up for the purposes of mass extermination as were the extermination camps.

Einsatzgruppen
The extermination squads of the SS used in the Russian campaign of 1941 with orders to shoot Communist Party officials, resisters and Jews.

Extermination camps
These camps, of which Auschwitz is the most notorious, were set up in Poland during the Second World War to carry out the mass extermination of the European Jews of whom six million are thought to have died. Other groups of people, of whom the gypsies were the most numerous, were also murdered in these camps.

Fascism
A new political ideology that gained much support in Europe in the period between the two world wars and formed the basis of several governments. Fascism believed in a mystical union of the national community under a strong leader. It preached the need for aggressive war, for personal hardness and heroism and, very often, for purity of the race. Fascist states aimed at a total control over people's lives and thoughts to be achieved through propaganda and terror. Germany under Hitler and Italy under Mussolini were Fascist Dictatorships. There are several regimes around the world today which have been compared to Fascist states and a number of neo-Fascist movements in Europe.

Führer
The German word for leader or guide. Hitler

54 Jews, liberals and socialists at Sachsenhausen concentration camp line up before the guards to hand over their civilian clothes.

was often addressed as the Führer and at the heart of Nazism was the idea of a divinely inspired leader. Society was to be based on leadership at all levels — this was known as the "leader principle".

German Workers' Party
A small political grouping, founded in Munich in January 1919, one of many new groups at the time, that preached a confused mixture of nationalism and socialism and was led by Anton Drexler. Hitler joined this party as its seventh committee member in September 1919 and the Nazi Party sprang from it, but traces of the original party were soon lost, especially of its socialist component.

Gleichschaltung
The process by which, in 1933 and 1934, the Nazis brought previously independent organizations within the umbrella of the Nazi movement. For instance, the previous youth movements became part of the Hitler Youth.

Hitler Youth
The Nazi youth organization. When the Nazis came into power they suppressed the independent and the Christian youth movements, and in the later years of the regime all German young people were forced to join the Hitler Youth where systematic training was given in Nazi ideology and soldiering.

Lebensraum
Living space. A specifically Nazi idea, the theory of Lebensraum was that the superior

race, the Aryans, had a need as a strong race to expand their frontiers and especially at the expense of the inferior "races" of eastern Europe. Taken seriously by some at the time, this idea seems totally irrelevant to us now.

NSDAP — Nationalsozialistische Deutsche Arbeiter Partei

The Nazi Party. In full, National Socialist German Workers' Party. Its main symbols were the swastika or hooked cross and the characteristic salute. The shortening "Nazi" was originally a contemptuous nickname, but became generally adopted.

New Order

The Nazi term for the carrying out of their policies, especially racial policies, over Europe as a whole, but especially in eastern Europe.

Reichstag

The German directly elected Parliament from 1871 to 1933, remaining as a powerless body within the Third Reich.

Right-wing and Left-wing

These two terms originally rose from the order of seating in the French Parliament during the French Revolution: the left wing wanted to carry the revolution further; the right wing wanted things to remain closer to what they had previously been. The two terms can be confusing and even shade into each other, but left-wing thought is now generally identified with socialism and its more extreme form, communism, and preaches public ownership of the means of production and social equality. Right-wing thought is identified with conservatism and also in the twentieth century, and more in economic than in social thought, with liberalism, the idea that people should have substantial control over their own lives and property. Nationalism and racism, in the twentieth century, have generally been part of extreme right-wing thought. Nazism was basically an extreme right-wing movement, although

some ideas, the idea of a national community of all classes, for instance, bear some resemblances to left-wing ideas.

SA — Sturmabteilung

(Stormtroopers). Originally simply bands of young fighters, later a virtual Nazi private army, led by Ernst Röhm. After 1934, when the main SA leaders were shot, the SA remained but was relatively powerless, its functions in the organization of terror being taken over by the SS.

SS — Schutzstaffel

(Bodyguard). Originating as Hitler's personal bodyguard in 1925, the SS, under Heinrich Himmler, developed into the Nazi terror organization. In the Third Reich the SS developed a wide variety of functions and became the chief vehicle of the extremism of Nazi racial policy. By the end of the war, with police, intelligence, planning and fighting functions, the SS had almost become a "state within a state".

Slavs

A population group living in eastern Europe and with closely related languages. The Nazis regarded Slavs as sub-human, although often, as Germans, they would have had Slav blood themselves.

Third Reich

Name often given to Nazi rule 1933-45. It was held that there had been two previous *Reiche* in German history: a medieval empire and the German monarchical empire lasting from 1871 to 1918. However, Germany has often been called a Reich throughout history when it has been a united state with imperial ambitions.

Totalitarianism

A tendency within twentieth-century states for the state apparatus to become so powerful and dictatorial that total control is achieved over the lives of citizens. State and society

thus become the same thing. It can be disputed how much this is ever achieved in practice, but certainly Nazi Germany as well as several communist states have approached this state of affairs.

Versailles Treaty
Main treaty signed in 1919 to end the First World War. The treaty emphasized the idea of self-determination of nations and set up many new republics out of ancient multinational empires. But it was often felt to have been over-harsh to defeated nations. Resentment at the treaty in Germany was one factor which helped the Nazis to power.

Völkischer Beobachter
(Racial Observer). The Nazi newspaper from early days, purchased for a small sum of money in 1919 when it was just an anti-semitic scandal sheet. The paper continued to publish during the whole Nazi period and during the war gave a notably inaccurate version of events.

Weltanschauung
(World Outlook). A German philosophical term for a coherent philosophy or outlook to explain all events; Nazism claimed to offer such a thing to its believers. It offered belief in Hitler as a divinely inspired leader, belief in authority and foreign conquest, belief in the national community and in the Germans as a superior race. In reality, Nazism was a confused hotch-potch of ideas, its main beliefs were prejudices, and its only real principle was a ruthless greed for power.

55 Hitler in an open car takes the march-past of the SA Stormtroopers.

Some Suggestions for Further Reading

Bullock, Alan   *Hitler: A Study in Tyranny* (Odhams 1952, Pelican Books 1962)

Fest, Joachim   *Hitler* (translation from German, Pelican Books 1977)

Shirer, William L.   *The Rise and Fall of the Third Reich* (Secker and Warburg 1960, Pan Books 1964)

Trevor-Roper, H.R.   *The Last Days of Hitler* (Macmillan 1947, Pan Books 1952)

Waite, Robert L.   *The Psychopathic God* (Basic Books 1977)

Index